POETRY NOW

BEACHCOMBINGS

Edited by Kerrie Pateman

First published in Great Britain in 1994 by
POETRY NOW
1-2 Wainman Road, Woodston,
Peterborough, PE2 7BU

FOREWORD

Although we are a nation of poetry writers we are accused of not reading poetry and not buying poetry books: after many years of listening to the incessant gripes of poetry publishers, I can only assume that the books they publish, in general, are books that most people do not want to read.

Poetry should not be obscure, introverted, and as cryptic as a crossword puzzle: it is the poet's duty to reach out and embrace the world.

The world owes the poet nothing and we should not be expected to dig and delve into a rambling discourse searching for some inner meaning.

The reason we write poetry (and almost all of us do) is because we want to communicate: an ideal; an idea; or a specific feeling. Poetry is as essential in communication, as a letter; a radio; a telephone, and the main criteria for selecting the poems in this anthology is very simple: they communicate.

Faced with hundreds of poems and a limited amount of space, the task of choosing the final poems was difficult and as editor one tries to be as detached as possible (quite often editors can become a barrier in the writer-reader exchange) acting as go between, making the connection, not censoring because of personal taste.

In this volume around two hundred and thirty poems are presented to the reader for their enjoyment.

The poetry is written on all levels; the simple and the complex both having their own appeal.

The success of this collection, and all previous *Poetry Now* anthologies, relies on the fact that there are as many individual readers as there are writers, and in the diversity of styles and forms there really is something to please, excite, and hopefully, inspire everyone who reads the book.

CONTENTS

BASTARD LIFE

My father was born into the arms
of mother without instinct,
Abandoned on the cold stone
floor of loss,
Where cruel piercing cries of
bastard ring,
From lips without movement
and eyes that glare.

Skeletons in the kubby hole
find truth,
Lonely lost boy living in hell,
Roaming the docklands,
For courage,
Searching the oceans,
For dreams,
Running from childhood,
Never received,
Toying with genuine hearts,
For unknown love,
Marriage, death, no dreams.

On that street now,
The homes torn down,
Where you grasped your chest,
And made that frown,
The road remains for all to see,
From its black tar oozes memory,
Inches square that bruised your skin,
Seeps through my heart,
And deep deep within,
Above this spot where your
Last breath fell,
I feel the dead part of me is well.

Adrian Fox

FAREWELL

Sometimes that smile carried more than words.
That whispering, little laugh,
The boyish, glinting face
Carved from the finest ivory:
Deathly white
Yet, oh so alive!

'Hold me,' you said.
So we clung close, warm
Safe, secure in love
And you sung in my ear
'I love you,' so that
All I could do was speak
The truth.
'I love you always.'

How has it come to this?
I love you, but goodbye
Is on my lips.
Stammering, shambolic sentences
Through my tear strained eyes.
Your lips quiver
Suppressing what I feel
And that last, final touch of your soft cheek,
The final embrace,
So much more than one of passion.
This is all I want,
One final farewell?

Kevin Hylands

WE HAVE NO CHOICE

I thought we kept no secrets, but I was wrong once again,
You are my lover, my confidante and my friend.
But O God how you've changed in my tired eyes,
And now I see no point in wearing a disguise.
We could continue, but it just wouldn't be the same,
And I don't want to be a part of a deceitful game.
Tonight you destroyed me, and I mean you tore me apart,
After you told me and said those surprising hurtful remarks.
Maybe you do not understand why I feel so strong,
But what I know now to continue would be so wrong.
I do love you, but what's in the future for us,
Maybe God will guide us in our separate lives, I trust.
I don't ever want to hurt you, I pray God will guide you with care,
How could we be as before when now I know, our lives just
                                    couldn't compare.
It's breaking my heart to face reality and live without you,
I couldn't love anyone as I love you, but heartbreak is nothing new.
You opened my eyes tonight to something that never crossed
                                    my mind,
But the real truth is that from our relationship I must decline.
I think shock has caused this decision, yet later I will agree,
No matter what happens forthwith, you will always be a part of me.
I'm not leaving because of what happened in your past,
Now you will never see me smile, unless it is a mask.
I love you because I know you as you are, at present,
And I can't complain because my memories are all pleasant.
I don't think you'll ever understand why I have decided to go,
Also the reasons behind my decision, you and I will never know,
If you could only hear my heart, and not listen to my voice,
You would know why we have to finish, because we have no choice.

Eilis Dowd

FASTRACK RELIGION

Lord, save us from fastrack religion,
You know just what I mean.
Those television preachers
Who crawl out of the screen.
You hear the words they're saying,
(What they're thinking you can't feel.)
Just peddlers of heaven in an earthbound property deal.

'Just send ten dollars in the mail . . .
Do it right away!
There's a treasury in heaven, a Big G Takeaway!
So claim it, get the interest too . . .
Don't wait 'til judgement day.
Your cheque will build a bigger, brighter temple to His name . . .
To centre in the Theme Park Scene,
A place I'll call *God's Kingdom Dream* . . .
It'll be wonderful!
(Saints will come from all over to pay to see it . . .)
And in this place, for sure, you'll see Isaiah's vision too,
The lion and the lamb laid down,
The peaceful, verdant grass to chew together. Ah . . . men!
(Special effects by Spielberg's crew . . .)
And snakes and lizards reconciled to live with little child . . .
(Could be difficult to animate . . .)
Will in this new creation with Him in glory, undefiled, forever stay.
(But this will all cost money and who'll write the soundtrack for the
                                                                angels?)

So send ten dollars in the mail, do it right away!
Believe me, trust me . . . God won't fail!
It's absolutely true!
Believe *Me*, trust *Me* . . . God won't fail!
There's a pact-of-plenty there for you!
(Me too . . . especially!)

So send ten dollars in the mail,
And get on board that fastrack *Kingdom* trail . . .
And do it right away . . . Ok?
(Lord there's one born every minute . . .)
God bless you all! . . . Ah . . . men!'

Alan Meacock

RECEPTION

Once upon a time . . .
A jungle of innocence,
Entrenched casualties with social sores.
They are impressionable,
but without an impression

of the

W o r l d.

Of the danger.
Cheap thrills,
ills, pills, bills
and you must provide the gills
through which they may
b
  r
    e
      a
        t
          h
            e.

The pillar.
Hide the wounds, make December June
so
everyone lived happily ever after.

Tim Whawell

PROLOGUE OF THE RICH BEGGAR

Innocent Dan did not know what to expect;
Born of rich upper class, he deemed respect
      Only child of Mr and Mrs Niminsky
      Educated at Oxford University,
      He was tops in every subject
   Amorous feat defeated his object
Lack of ambition he baffled his tutors.

Righteous friends ridicule his actions
Clever but subtle, he has no intention
Of succumbing to trends of his generation
A nine to five job is out of the question.
His parents made plans for his immigration
   That to him is flawed with irritation
   Astute to hinder their every movement
Fine houses, fast cars, his involvement.

      A country home, suburban villa
      He plans to marry his Anabella;
      Date is set, town house acquired
Invitations printed, a gilt edge as required,
      His bride to be a glamorous minor
Freckles girl two-timing with a miner;
      Vulgar maid, great pretender.
Up and leave, run off, what a scandal!

As gossip spread his inner thoughts tremor
   Dan's world collapse, he's in a stupor
His plans are wrecked, wild, bewildered,
Inspirations gone, zilch-ambition inflated,
   Defeatist fashion stem this to trigger
He necessitate the road, spineless beggar.

Chauffeur driven to an office block
He change in tatters to do his lot;
    His poster reads,
    'Help the poor,
    Homeless and hungry,
    Sleeping on the moor.'
    Returning to his stately home
  Dan Niminsky, thrifty beggar, pour
Champagne to bribe his conniving staff
They drink their full but label him
          'Dam, sickening and daft.'

Zeedy Thompson

DISTINCT MEMORY

'Rip strike'
Knowing where I began makes a difference,
This is my life.
Where it's gone tomorrow, who knows or even cares,
I realise what I'm doing is all you may have been.
  No questions only the truth is hidden,
      I remember you, we saw life at the same time,
But not with equal eyes.
  I once felt scared of you, I felt you liked it that way?
To be your little puppet and slave.
Don't worry I always admired you no matter what.
      Tonight we recollected and related -
Only because I'm now the age you were.
  I am a stupid human being for becoming what my parents created.
      I often felt slightly disgusted by your other ways.
Show me the way to the white,
I know of those who've seen it - no way back.
Nothing in particular affected me the same way,
Does this force me to be alone?
          'I knew when it came but was unsure of how to -
          Stop it all.'
Julie Ann Devon

7

MINER'S BOY

I have doused the sun,
cannot speak the reason.

When I went down my first day
the sky was shut.
I stroked my new moleskins
and was proud.
'They'll not shine so
come end of shift,'
Gwyn said.

The cage dropped
and the wind screamed.
I never knew such dark -
it crawled over my scalp;
I thought I would choke.
'Hold on to your stomach!'
called Gwyn
and I swallowed down my fear.

When snap-time came
I looked for Gwyn,
could not find him.
A man I did not know
took me by the arm.
'Come you!'

He led me into a black tunnel
away from the other men.
'Bluebells! I can smell -'
'Hold your tongue, boy!'

When I came up to pit-top
at end of shift
it was night.
My trousers did not shine.
Each day it is the same.

When I remember
my insides leap and throb,
my face burns.
I am glad they cannot see.

Now I am a man
and God cannot stand
to look on me.

Liz Arden

TORN CURTAIN

The curtain so brilliant
        White and starched
Was a symbol of pride
For people who passed the window
        From near and far.

When I was a child
        Not one finger I dared
Touch the lace
Or seeing it out of place.
That was my mother's
        Pride and joy.

Now with a broken heart
I stand and stare.
That once beautiful curtain
        Hanging there,
All torn and grey
        And neglect so.

As I return now I know
        The reason why
That beautiful curtain
        So torn and sad.
My mother has gone
        Without saying goodbye.

Agnes Solan

9

THE FLOWER SELLER

A figure hurries down the street,
With basket, hat and tattered shawl,
And worn down shoes upon her feet,
Trudges to her steps and wall.

For years she's sold her flowers gay,
And sung her song of old,
To everyone who passed her way,
The words would all unfold.

'Come buy my flowers my pretty ones,
Come one, come two, or all,
Come buy from Meg, my handsome gents,
As I sit here, by my wall.'

Her eyes still shine, but tired now,
Her back is round and bent,
Love of life is passing her by,
Her life is almost spent.

Alas, the winter took its toll,
And Meg is here no more,
And folk are sad that they can't hear,
Flower seller Meg, as before.

'Come buy my flowers, my pretty ones,
Come one, come two, or all,
Come buy from Meg, my handsome gents,
As I sit here, by my wall.'

Audrey Shepherd

HALOED

Tonight in half darkness
watching from a train window
The mountains have haloes,
Against the red sky.

If I was a shepherd I would be delighted,
To see that the saints are here,
In the sad land.
In the Sad Land,
we are caught in a long sleep,
as if,
in faces we see others we knew before,
looking back at us,
seeing faces they knew before,
as if
our dreams have caught up with our waking lives.

Tiny small fires kindle
in our sleepwalkers eyes
Blood red flowers,
The gift of tears.

Maria Pavledis

CARE IN THE COMMUNITY

With a smile as empty
As a new dug grave
The counsellor
Picks over the leavings
Of one he is paid to help.

Adopts a position
The correct body language
And makes a point -
Puts his victim in his place.

Gordon Strong

11

SO THAT NO ONE SHOULD FORGET THE HUMAN TRAGEDY

*In the summer of 1991, a soldier returned home to find his wife and
two young children dead in their cottage. The mother had died of
heart failure, leaving the babies unable to fend for themselves.
Villagers assumed that they were staying with relatives.*

So that no one should forget the human tragedy
They made it clearly sensational,
The media took it, but found it small
And too frail,
The story simply sad,
No cruelty
Just life and death pretending to be bad.

  Daddy come and help me I am alone,
  I'm hungry and my head hurts
  My hands are cold as stone,
  I'm blinded in this prison, I want my doll,
  Oh my god I'm grown up
  And I'm in hell.

  I hear you call across the water
  Tiny daughter,
  Your tears bleed into my heart with no love wanting,
  How could I know your pain was real
  And not another nightmare,
  How could I help the way you had to take
  How could I.

  I took a job with prospects, tried to be
  The perfect father to my family,
  How I wish that I had not been born,
  How I wish that we all had not been born.

No one was responsible in the end
They said it was natural causes,
'We keep ourselves to ourselves,' a neighbour told the press,
'Living remote,
They'd gone away to visit,
We thought,'
Instead they all lay dying bit by bit.

Helen Lane

MEN FROM OUTER SPACE

We are the Folk from Outer Space, we'd like to visit Earth,
If you'd give us time and place, and tell us where to berth,
We've circled 'round for years and years, a-frightened for to land,
Frightened of you Earth Folk, who'd come with sword in hand.

You think that we are monsters, but that is not quite so,
We're waiting on the right time, our secrets for to show,
We have no guns, or deadly gear, our aim is peace, we swear,
There's many untrue stories about us in the air.

So if you see our saucers, please just keep calm and cool,
We are not out to harm you, we have a real strict rule,
We are not out to destroy, our task is to assist,
So please don't be frightened, when we come thru' the mist.

Our rule is not to frighten, or put you to distress,
We only want to help you, clear up the world's mess,
Please don't get excited, our task will never cease,
We'll circle 'round your troubled world, with helping hands of peace.

So when you see our space ships, please do not make a fuss,
We'd welcome all you Earth Folk to come and visit us,
We are harmless people, from a million miles away,
And when you folk accept us will be a happy day.

Jimmy Sinclair

DIFFERENT WORLDS

So you think you lead the hard life,
and fate's been cruel to you,
that you deserve a little more from life,
boy have I got news for you.

You complain you really work too hard,
what you have is mere existence,
now you're having second thoughts,
fear you may not go the distance.
And this is your first holiday,
for years and years and years,
divert this plane a few degrees,
I'll show you a vale of tears.

You'll see some accommodation,
you *would* write and complain about,
where they've never seen a water tap,
and whole families die of drought.
A land where the nearest water,
is a three hour walk away,
so think of that, while you're smugly sat,
on your shiny white bidet.

There is no pretty air hostess,
to serve Them from a tray,
that meal you think so tiny,
would feed a family for a day.
You whinge about the flight delay,
how it's ruined your holiday timing,
when the engine sounds have died away
no doubt you'll still be whining.

We're landing at Nairobi soon,
Mogadishu's a little farther,
there children fight for grains of rice,
wear flies as living mascara.
You're reading in the flight mag,
about the latest diet plan,
put down your drink, just stop and think,
and imagine if you can.

Imagine a child with matchstick legs,
and grotesque distended belly,
y'know the ones that you switch over from,
when you see them on the telly.
This child has parents just like you,
they feel, they hope, they cry,
if we don't stretch out a helping hand,
well mostly they'll just die.

Can I just ask something,
and see if you agree?
Are we born with an obligation?
Or do we just live duty free?

Peter K Church

BEDFONT

I'll not want
To go to the village of Bedfont
To the place there, I have been
Peacocks live there, seldom seen
Plenty live there, that there are
most though see it from their car
Planes cross over in the sky
Noise and fumes pass as they fly
Poor old village, I'll not want
To be a place called Bedfont

A C Tilson

OLD AGE

Daylight beckons
  birds chorus.
All sleep banished,
  she wakes.
Another day.

Doorbell rings,
  she must rise.
'Tis the milkman,
  a contact.
Asks, 'Is she well?'

The joints ache,
  and creak.
'Arthritis,' they say,
  with zimmer
She shuffles around.

No need to hurry,
  nor fret.
No responsibilities beckon,
  just sit,
Long hours remembering.

Again the bell,
  meals on wheels.
'How are we today?
  must eat, whilst hot,'
They say.

Ambulance calls,
  an outing.
To old folks' club
  transported.
Confused she sits, listens.

Kindly lady
  brings tea.
Steadies the shaking hand,
  she sips.
Under the caring gaze.
Home again, the chair beckons,
  she sits.
The book beckons,
  she reads,
But the page blurs.

May E Ireland

IT'S THERE SOMEWHERE

It happens when I'm on the phone,
Also when I'm deep in thought,
Or if I'm left to be alone,
This compulsion I have fought.

I've tried not to do this thing,
I've done it nearly all my life,
Even though the pleasure it can bring,
I know it will get me into strife.

It starts off small and slow,
And logic goes out of the door,
This thing just seems to grow,
Then there's no space anymore.

There's no beginning and no end,
No clue to what it is,
So with every message that I send,
You also get a doodle quiz.

For somewhere on the page, just there,
Amongst the patterns that I shape,
You may have to sit and stare,
The words are waiting to escape.

Lorraine Lowndes

17

DAUGHTERS

A mixture of joy, a type of madness
Sometimes anger, and even sadness
It was for little girls, I was yearning
They came without a written warning
I thanked the Lord I'd had my wish
My girls were another kettle of fish
They kept me going day and night
And sometimes I never ate a bite
In the garden they built their den
They added their gang of nine or ten
Parties were added, squabbles galore
Appointed me Ref, I could keep score
Soon it was history, I wondered 'what's next'
Gained a keen interest in the opposite sex
Never knew what trouble was till then
Just kept repeating, 'Be home here for ten,'
Few boys they brought home seemed suited
And sometimes in turn, my girls did dispute it
I'd argue that I could see, and was wise
That love always shone in loving couples' eyes
Well my girls and I have kept the pace
We stood together, we finished the race
And looking back, they were happy days
The love, the laughter, time can't erase
My daughters, they're fine women now
We'll always care, we made that vow
And I feel that now in my serenity
They're My Faith, Hope, and My Charity . . .

Maura T Bye

RUDE AWAKENINGS

They came in the night.
Scavengers.
They smashed the locks.
Removed the front screen.
Dented the doors,
Wrenched out the radio and escaped.
Unheard. Unseen.

In the morning,
Whilst urging my small son to hurry,
For fear of being late for school,
I saw,
No reflection of the low morning light,
But an emptiness where the screen had been.
A rain splattered teddy trampled in the mud.
A cassette crushed under an uncaring foot.
And we wept.

I drive now.
No radio.
No invitation. No temptation.
But we sing, my son and I.
In stereo.
A Christmas Carol. A Nursery Rhyme.
Snatches of Rogers and Hammerstein.
Out of tune. Miss a line.
We sing.
But I weep inside,
For my child has seen,
That base side of mankind.

But as the policeman said.
'It happens all the time.'

Christine Pearce

NOT GUILTY

You've got the wrong person,
Please can't you see.
I was only shopping.
For my family's tea.

Why lock me up?
I really won't harm.
I'm not violent.
Take your hand from my arm.

I can't face this cell,
It's really too small.
Don't shut the door.
Please hear my call.

Why am I here?
What have I done?
I'm not a thief,
I'm not the one.

The walls closing in,
I really can't breathe.
Open a window.
Take your hand from my sleeve.

The walls getting closer,
I'm perspiring like hell,
Please! Please!
Let me out of this cell.

Violent you say,
That's really not me.
Please go away,
You're annoying me.

Oh! now I've done it.
This is going to be hell.
Locked permanently,
Inside this prison cell.

Ellen Marshall

SOFT SOAP ADVERT

and now
take off your warm gloves
and wash your hearts with *Might!*

Might is right
for you
for me
for us
use it with pride!
day and night
'cause
Might is right!
always has been
always will be

why is it right?
asked one of the bright

don't be contrite
lonely, dim light
wash your mouth out and listen:
it doesn't matter anymore who's right
wrong
or ding dong
if you use *Might* daily
and national pride for the rough patches
you are winning the dirt game
alright?

Alfa

WAITING

Tick-tock, tick-tock
That's all I hear.
The sound of the clock.
Pitter-patter, pitter-patter
The splash of rain
Down my window pane.
Children playing.
Laughing. Crying.
Don't they know. I'm here -
Dying.

Old and tired. My body's
Bent. And wracked with pain.
Each day I wait -
And hope. In vain.
Someone will call
As they pass by.
Before I die.

My wrinkled face
Is worn and haggered.
Is it because of that
No one is bothered.
Will I be found -
There'll be no sound.
When I die.

The days are long
And weary now.
Emptiness fills my head.
Cold. Alone. And frightened.

I wait.
To die.
In bed.
That's all I hear
The sound of the clock,
Tick-tock, tick-tock . . .

Doreen Jones

FREEDOM IN THE WIND

Blackness as the Harley Davidson throbs through the night
A rider originals, a tatter, no helmet.
      That is my right.
Moonlight glinting on the raked, front forks naked as day.
The hog and rider asexual together,
      King of all they survey.
Wind pounding in the ears, hair streaming,
      Freedom in the darkness at last.
Non baffled, hog, noise, excitement, but am I going too fast,
But what does it matter, I'm the law, I'm elite
      I have the right.
To travel in freedom, blood pounding, so free in the night,
I know my time will come.
      When I'm riding alone on my hog.
But oh! To ride the roads of hope, alive mind free of fog
The end is coming to this dark rider
      Of the wind
Is he guilty of wanting to ride free. Has he really sinned,
A crack of thunder, suddenly roars
      Road awash, then an almighty flash,
A wobble violent snaking, a pylon oh God! What a crash
The dark rider will now ride at last today free
      In the sky with no fog,
With his hair streaming in the eternal wind,
      On his eternal hog.

Valerie Taylor

THE SUREST WAY TO STOP SMOKING

So, you've made up your mind to fight
Your long-lasting smoking habit?
Well, let's start. I'll help you. All right?

What? Your last one? Just for tonight?
No! No, no! Start right now. Do sit;
I can well understand your plight.

Man, you're fidgeting. Don't! Sit tight!
Take out your packet . . . and light. That's it.
Thanks. Look at me. Keep looking bright!

Now, with your left hand, hold your right.
Here's one of your own fags. Eat it!
Part your lips, Man. Not so . . . just slight.

Place it between your teeth. Now, bite.
Chew! Once . . . and twice . . . and thrice. Repeat!
Good. Got the art. You're great, quite!

Now, swallow it! No need for fright!
Open your mouth. It's not there. Right,
You *are* already cured of smoking. Alight!

What's it? You're asking if I might
Tell you what stuff I put in it?
Well, some cockroach shit. That's all. Christ!?

Anyway, my friend, that was my mite
To help you quit your smoking habit!
As fees, I'll just keep your fags and light!

Kopan Mahadeva

24

ASHWELL VILLAGE

Leaving London far behind
I travelled on the Cambridge line
Away from all the smoke and grime,
Feeling better all the time.

Ashwell Station arrived at last.
I left the train and, walking fast,
I made my way through fields of green
To the prettiest village I'd ever seen.

The parish church has a crooked spire
(After Agincourt they made it higher).
If you know where to look, on one of the walls
You can see an engraving of Old St Pauls.

Down the High Street you will find
Pleasures of a different kind.
Delicious cakes and fresh baked bread.
The best in Hertfordshire, 'tis said.

The Springs in Ashwell are the source
Of the River Cam, and there, of course,
Deep in the water, it's been confirmed,
Is where you can find the Ice Age Worms.

Although the village may be old
There's new development, I'm told,
Which blends in well with cottage and barn
At the end of the High Street at Westbury Farm.

There are farms to see with pigs and cows,
A museum nearby where one can browse.
There's so much to see, so much to do.
I'll come back again. How about you?

Betty E Lockwood

'THINK' THINK AGAIN

The sickening feeling of trying for that last effort,
Struggling in vain?
For good health thrown away
That will not come again.

The darkening thoughts like dying day
Clutching at the air,
But hope that is not there.
For good health thrown away -
The desperate plea
'Give me one last chance and I'll repay.'

But the onward marching time
Days towards who knows what, God's plan?
The time one never thought to see
But comes to every man.

Oh God of all forgiveness
Lift my thoughts to thee,
And give me hope that my last days
Worthless will not be.

Give me the courage and the strength
To lift the fallen from the floor,
Even though death itself is knocking at my door.

And make my poor tired body
Glad, humble and grateful too,
That you have given this humble man
More than he was due.

And make me truly humble when,
I remember some sweet thing of two
Was plucked from earth to paradise,
And did not have his due.

My chance to me was given,
I knew it from the start,
You gave me strong good organs
Good teeth, strong lungs, stout heart.

But smoking was my downfall,
I pooh! Poohed! All I'd heard,
But now how I wish I'd heeded,
Every single word.

That treacherous weed,
How many more
Will it pull slowly to death's door,
And tiny tot of only two
With sweetie cigarette held up to you,
Think, think again
Taboo taboo.

Ann Rosalind Roberts

CABINET CULTURES

Good causes made
Conspirators all

No memos sent
To reach due ends

A look, a breath,
The blood within their veins

Thick with
Conspired moves

Their targets understood
No message to reprove

Back-slapped package
Balanced UK books.

John Comerford

FEELINGS

Sad clouds whispered,
crossed the sky.
White rose wafting scent
stung my soul.
I cried,
'I love you.'

Fading light shone
its final beam,
curtsied out of sight
as I cried,
'I love you.'

Street's dying sounds
silenced into night.
Owls hoot.
Slivered moon strains secure
on dark sea.
Black night
pulsated bated breath
against heaving breast
and I cried,
'I love you.'

Smell of dampened
earthy dust,
rain warmed,
filled my mind
and like two lovers
sucked it in,
love saturated,
drowsy drunk
and still I cried,
'I love you.'

June Brenton

28

FREEDOM ONCE MORE

I lie in my death bed, dead;
No patterns of remorse in my head.
I'm not stung by your lies,
Nor bound by your ties;
I'm not moving or thinking, I'm dead.

I could never believe in your pain;
I won't have the chance now again.
And for that I am glad,
You were driving me mad,
And now you must live with my shame.

I was never quite sure of your wishes;
Your cold, hollow eyes were so vicious.
I hated your smile,
It just struck me as vile,
Each expression was purely malicious.

To you, I was merely dead skin;
I was nothing, I could never win.
So you slashed through my brain,
Just to wrack me with pain,
And never once thought of your sin.

Your orders were always so twisted;
You despised me so, when I resisted.
When I refused once again,
You went madly insane
And my eyes went so dull as you fisted.

So I lie in my death bed, dead;
No patterns of remorse in my head.
I'm not stung by your lies,
Now you're bound with my ties,
I'm not moving, you're thinking, I'm dead.

Andrew Bartlett

IMMORTALITY

If life is just a passing show with nothing at its end
And Paradise a myth, does mere oblivion descend?
Are family ties and love and friendship gone for evermore
Or carried on eternally in Heaven's boundless store?

Great preachers, learned scholars, and the faiths of countless creeds
Use immortality's appeal to nourish mankind's needs
But sometimes doubt besets us all, and many truths we miss
Through pondering what great divide might mar eternal bliss

Agnostics, atheists, and fools continually decry
All hopes of everlasting life, as life spans hurry by
Supported by some brilliant minds who justify such views
With lengthy obtuse arguments that baffle and bemuse

In spite of this the human race seems so detached and cold
To seeking immortality through means they're often told

The manner of our going, and the lifetime path we trod
Cannot deny or challenge the validity of God
Supreme divine Creator of the wonders we can see
And countless basic natural laws of skilful mystery

Can anyone who contemplates life's marvellous romance
Believe that all these wonders come upon us by mere chance?

Kenneth W White

BAD PATCH

Your voice is dull and very far away.
At the first careful coolness I can see
the mood you summoned when you woke today
was one denying any need of me.

I realise rejection and become
resigned that we will hurt each other now
each by the other's silence as we shun
what each is to the other, knowing how

30

we have before, and speaking still I turn
my heart away - it's struggle is its own
of self-accusing sorrow. I am torn
between us, and no tremble in your tone

will give your soul away, and none in mine
- polite, impassive strangers, chanced to meet,
whose empty conversation never quite
betrays a flicker of the flame beneath.

Fran Ward

THE PURPOSE OF EXISTENCE

Not a single human being, individual, alive,
in these fifty thousand years of his evolution,
from the monkey to twenty-first century space rockets,
looking for the purpose of our individual existence, and
combined existence, by searching the furthest confines of space,
is able to say precisely what is the purpose of existence.
Sure there are many myths and fables that teach us,
that if we're evil to our contemporary human beings,
that there are retributions awaiting us in the afterlife;
can't see that this is true, but if we get on with
the business of surviving, being as kind as possible to others
who come into contact with us, then we have nothing to
fear in this life, or whatever happens when we die,
as we've tried to live as peaceably as possible with
other individual human beings, their families, tribes, and nations.
Politics, eventually, doesn't count for much,
it could always have been less brutal, more compassionate,
and some live in the lap of material luxury,
while the others dream of it, therefore the hard edge
of politics is lodged in brutality, more's the pity, so be it.
Spiritually, I suppose only a buddhist monk is at one,
with the present, with his God, but even he prays
elaborately to an unknown entity.

Robin Williams

LAST BUS

Nocturnal winds
Raid with gusts
And ghosts of dust
Shadows for the paranoid
Streets
Empty as sleep
Hushed

Nothing moves except
tears of fear
on a young woman's
cheeks, as an old man,
drunk, explains his desire
to kiss. Hidden by the shelter
his shadow cloaks her
misted pleading. No,
she cannot go, she waits.

'Yer a braw lookin' lass,'
His parlance wavering,
slavering, 'just one for
an old man.'
Hideously frightened, her
claret depths tight and
verging on a shriek or
whimper, but the injured
attract a lion. She waits.

Already half fact,
the fear in the act
of becoming real,
a beast being born
in the shadow.

Slow birthpain seeping,
rearing up, flashing.
A flood of fact, staring
with lolling eyes, speaking
spittle and bitter breath.

Then, a halo, a bright ring
'round his head. Two bright
spots emerge, like angels' essence.
And, drawing out her arm,
bringing it down in a bright flash,
she slashes the cord.
Bursts it,
shatters it, scatters it.
Severed, into awry night the old drunk
goes,
gone
to bury his stillborn basilisk in the
throes of
dawn.

Scott McKenzie

THE DANGERS OF SUPERSTITION

Sheltering under a tree -
In a thunderstorm, she said:
'The things that have happened to me
          (Touch wood)
It's a wonder I'm not dead.'
Flash! Bang! 'You've died,'
Her friend replied.
'And so, my dear, you see,
It's not too good
To touch the wood
When lightning strikes the tree.'

Allan Wrigley

COMMUTER

So what are you thinking
As you sit there on the bench seat?
Clean shaven, crisp shirt,
So very pressed and neat.

Where do your thoughts lie
As you travel on the train?
Grey-green country rushing past,
Blurring in the rain.

What occupies your mind
In your solitary isolation?
Bodies trying not to touch
With over compensation.

Could it be of tasks ahead?
Or loved ones left at home?
Train halts, we disembark,
I guess I'll never know.

Nicola Walker

ON THE COAST ROAD (NORTH ANTRIM)

The old couple speak of the storm
That stole some slates in the night
As they shuffle on to the bus
Stiffening to sit.
I see young friends flickering in their faces.
They look back to say, 'And take care.'
They make a ceremony of their stop.

We are going all the way to the country of the old,
Entranced by the sea in winter,
Where they stare at their own horizons
Nearing with every dying wave
That bears their ship-wrecked thoughts
And dips, finally, foaming into the sand.

Stephen Brown

FOR LONELINESS SAKE

I walk the streets with an excuse to buy
for human contact I need to make
the dull and listless look in my eye
is there because of loneliness sake.

My room is nice I hear people say
how comfy you must be
but little do they really know
the screaming that's inside of me.

For days on end I sit alone
with nothing but my thinking
until with tears I shout at the phone
my soul and spirits sinking.

I don't choose to behave like this
if only I could find a way
to change this life I nearly live
and wake with sunshine in my day.

But fate decrees that this is my
existence and I must
struggle on until such time
my body turns to dust.

I light another cigarette
and watch the world outside
then pour a drink and ruefully smile
because my world has died.

Month by month and year by year
the time drags on its sickly
there must be someone somewhere for me
I must find them soon and quickly.

I can take no more at last I find
my life means nothing but I don't moan
I take the pills and write this line
'Just one more lonely soul, gone home.'
Christopher M Holland

THE LIGHT

Death is but an end;
Life is but a shadow.
Momentary,
Insubstantial,
Flailing, foolishly against time's inevitable march.

Sorrow is but a flicker;
Love is yet a glimpse,
Elusive,
Perpetual,
Of the image, seen through a dream's mist, the shadow's
   meaning.

We try to grasp the intricacies of the pattern,
But who casts the shadow?

Juliet Ponsonby

BLOSSOM

Still she could not remember the blossom
Falling that spring. Though he told her later
Of its mosaic on the pond's surface
And in the half-light how she'd felt the same
Until it stuck to her raking fingers.
By day, she recalled, she'd roamed the staircase
Like a cat, her footfall growing lighter
As the time of his returning grew close.

But she could not remember the blossom
And of the season found nothing to say,
Not one syllable. And in years beyond
Their sight, old and alone, always the same
Likeness of her came to his sleep, the woods
Full of shadow, her kneeling by the pond,
And how she'd watched the blossom float away,
Shaking water from her fingers like words.

Ian Caws

THE TALE

Pattines in the morning sky
Roses drenched in silver dew
Eyes of beauty, wishful sigh
In the shadows hope renew;
Height of noon with sunshine blazing
Wrought the meadows sweet in May
Where the young ewe gently grazing
Came to prime in wondrous day;
Shadows falling, evening wonder
Purpling sky all gold inlaid
Made the poet cease to ponder
On the sonnet should it fade;
Fairy rings in shafts of moon
All dewy eyed till spell of morn'
Where the young winds rising soon
On golden alchemy are borne;
Heat of noon with shimmering haze,
Glorious sky in vivid hue
In that hush which came on golden days
When immortal sound on mortal grew;
When autumn sighed its sweet lament
And russet glow clad summer pride
And the drowsy bee its day well spent
Gave up its lease on all who died;
Joy still came in autumn dressed
To cast long shadows on the day
And lulled that hoary youth to rest
When winter came to prowl and prey
But winter out of autumn grew
And donned his icy mantle pale
To tread on all that joy made new
To make of all a wintry tale.

William Thomas Charlton

BORN TO FOLLOW

I feel I'm different from the rest,
An outcast left within,
A shadow on society,
A tolerated sin.

I watch them as they live their lives,
Replicas of their peers,
Generations of continuance,
Inheriting their fears.

Their minds lie swamped in apathy,
Only seeing what they're shown,
The pattern for their lives is set,
Their prejudices sown.

They've never questioned anything,
Their entire life's perception,
Dictated throughout childhood,
A lifetime of deception.

Born to follow leaders,
They sleep-walk through their days,
No inclination for the freedom,
They've had brainwashed away.

Wallowing in ignorance,
They live until they die,
But perhaps these fools are happier,
Then if they stopped to wonder why.

Graham Gillam

KAPUT

For F.

Stunned in the back of a car
racing among the neon flurry
of a city unknown.
Weakly sentimental: it all flooded to me . . .

Etching at my
glass-scrapings curling
from a needle pushed
along a window.

Splurging viscid goo immersed
my lungs as I yelled,
Ingredients of your tasks are
indecent, unpolished unyielding.

Eager for a masculine pastime
you greased the walk-way
and loosened the screws on the safety rail . . .
Confusing me by pampering my fractures.

Presenting you with clusters of petals
tempt you to sneeze
at a blessing of the girl
next door, next planet.

Urinating in some hedge,
a desperate picnicker can be
natural and so open.
'I never know when to keep my mouth shut.'

Winched to safety,
I cut the cable.

Austin Bonner

VISIONS

I lie upon my couch -
this to that idly pass -
thoughts go where they will
I hold the world with my grasp

Mother of blossoms and of all
Cradle of the earth also sky
dreaming - warm winds that play
clouds brightening - drift idly by

Streams run cool lazy way
green of fields - and trees
sweet birds sing - flitting free
these riches such as these

Is there anything so fair
pleasant moods - I lie here still
these all visions in my mind
passing hours at my will.

Mary Me-Lin

GHOSTS

A long interred and forgotten event
Breaks the surface of my mind,
An unexpected and unwanted resurrection,
An unsolicited reminder.
Memory pushes back the decades,
I am once again in my youth.
What happened then?
Nothing drastic, just an unhappy occurrence.
Do old sins cast long shadows?

Whilst I don't altogether believe in ghosts
I'm beginning to have the odd feeling
That I'm being slightly haunted.

Val Gordon

BANK HOLIDAY BLUES

Bank Holiday, and the sea calls,
The lonely hills and the sky,
To get far away from four walls,
And on my back to lie.

But what do I find on the road
That winds
Into the distance and over the lea?

Nose to tail at a snail's pace
Joining the holiday road race
Not an inch of space I see

Engines over-heating in traffic's
Crawling stream,
Exploding tempers shattering all dreams -
Of peace!
Bored children crying, exasperation
And sighing.

Every Bank Holiday it's the same,
Ironically, we play this game,
Why do we get this urge to roam,
We'd relax far more if we stayed
At home!

Doreen Shand

IF

If hope was a candle I'd light one every day
And give it to someone who was lost or gone astray
If love was a candle I'd burn it night and day
To show the world through love and hope there will always be a way
And if peace was a candle, I'd let the flame burn clear and strong
Till everyone could see that night will triumph over wrong.

Phyllis Sandiford

THE TRIANGLE

Reluctantly adjacent they sit
Sublimely critical of one another
Critical of the other's right
Critical of the other's attitude
Critical of the other's qualities

All because of her

They compare worthiness for her hand
Subconsciously
Subconsciously they stress their worthiness
Subconsciously they detest the other
Subconsciously they dream of eliminating
The other

All because of her

Irrational hatred sets in bringing
Insatiable contempt
Anger flourishes in both runners as their
Actions are held on a tight rein
Mentally unaccepting the situation they seek to
Physically destroy the obstacle
Outward signs of inner emotions are curbed by
Nonchalance

Nonchalantly they seem to outwardly accept the
Triangle
Both are anxious
Both are tense
Both are afraid

All because of her

Reluctantly she officiates
Knowing love does not accommodate
Divided feelings
Love is total or does not exist

She dare not think
She dare not speak
She dare not choose

Time becomes lethal as she waits
Dreading her decision

Undecided she sits
Undecided she decides
Decided
She weeps.

Ray Chapman

HOPE

When we're sad
we look to the past
and always wonder
why it didn't last

We laugh, we cry
we even hate
but if we're honest
it's down to fate

Don't think of the past
for that, it's too late
let's look to the future
and everything to date

I'm still on my own
sometimes it's hell
but you never know
what the future tells

But I yearn to be happy
one day it might be
if my dream comes true
someone will love me.

H A Fahey

FINAL SILENCE IN THE HIGH-PUBLICITY-TENSION-ZONE

       the sun sunk
on our silence
                for the last time
there was zero left to say
       the imminent dusk
and
    the cat-calls
        persecuting us
           said it all
I wanted
       a final touch (something!)
but it seemed so cheap
       with all the morons
            around us
       their blood-shot eyes
           giving us no rest
we walked back
    into the darkness
         followed by the sound
    of a thousand
        insolent feet
we were
     no longer one
        me and you
amongst the incessant strain
  of our final silence
     in the zone
         of no rest.

Amen.

Matthew Lee

UNTITLED

From heaven there came a woman giving joy and burning
light,
She offered gracious tendemess, scatt'ring shadows of
the night,
Her fire, her love, her wisdom charmed and warmed me to
the core,
Ecstasy unparalleled when she loved me on the floor.

Ardour cooled, love fled, my grieving heart was cursed
with so much pain,
I yearned for her and wished her thoughts of me could
be the same,
I pine, and pray the hurt will ease, for I know she
won't be mine,
But my floor gives me the mem'ry, of love's sordid
passion fine.

Michael Morris

ULTIMATE SEASONS!

The Children;

The splitting of many different particles of light;
Through the millions of barks
and hollows;
of aspen trees,

As he looks through-them in his coming years;
Of Life!
I try - to cope; to cope

To take care!
to be there,
and to be here.

I see many difficult reasons - to *Live!*
In the *Ultimate - Seasons!*

Peter Haydock

45

COMEUPPANCE

Rob was a bully, a terrible pest.
Causing annoyance was what he did best.
He'd heckle his teacher, her patience he'd try.
He'd punch the wee fellows and make the girls cry.

Then one day along came a timid wee thing,
Who happened to like to be happy and sing.
Rob wouldn't allow this, he started his games,
He tripped her and punched her and called her names.

The others stood watching, for they were afraid,
These days in the playground, nobody played,
You dare not complain, for things would get worse,
The atmosphere was terribly terse.

But Rob, like most bullies, had met his match,
With the timid wee thing, there was a catch.
She had a sharp tongue, and she knew how to hurt,
He ran away wiping his eyes on his shirt.

Now she was in charge, it has to be said.
A natural leader, the others she led.
This soon put an end to Rob's bullying way,
'She's put him in his place,' the kids would say.

Rob married his nemesis when they grew up!
People all said he deserved what he got.
But he seemed to be happy, he knew her so well,
Perhaps they were soul mates, who can tell?

Katy Connell

46

THE DOWNTRODDEN HEROES

On our streets we see them day by day,
Knights of the road hanging on to zero.
We watch, stare but don't really care,
For the life of the downtrodden hero.

> They live in life's shadow,
> In a world of nastiness
> To survive they beg or borrow,
> But are always penniless.

Plastic bags and cardboard boxes, are their home,
Onwards to nowhere finds only strife.
The penniless prince is forced to roam,
Where abuse and mockery is a way of life.

> They live in life's shadow,
> In a world of nastiness.
> For them there is only sorrow,
> And a life of homelessness.

Tired and forlorn they look as they travel along,
Shuffling their weary way between reality and hell.
The Queen has fallen, the King lives on,
To suffer more, too much to tell.

> They live in life's shadow,
> In a world of nastiness.
> For them there is no tomorrow,
> Only a life of loneliness.

Roy R Hackers

PURE ALPHABETISM

Attractive artistic activity
Benign balm
Comforting calm.
Deliveries, drear delirium,
Energises easy empathy.
Fulfils fantasy.

Great generosity.
Heady heedless
Ironic idioms.
Just.
Keeping.

Lacking love,
Mewling, maudlin.
New nonsense now.

Open ovation,
Porous, pathetic,
Quietly quizzing.

Rare refined,
Singing selective sonnets.
Taking trouble,
Unquestioned.
Valiant, vain,
Wasting words.

Excess.
Yes - unyielding.
Zaccharius.

M G E Demack

MISSING THE BOAT

The harbour I'm told to sail from
in sweet - sour dreams is all but dead
of ships. I watch long neglected quays
by a curtain, bordel red. One room,
bare floors, boards; how they waver
and sound to menace running up the stair.

Shaking - collar's loose, tie is far too long,
both shoelaces have gone - and trapped.
The evening ferry shrugs off the pier,
hung with tinplate signs of shipping lines,
household names now redundant in
precocious rust, past ageing wharves, yards,

cranes only wind will move, to the unblinking
lighthouse at the hidden river's mouth.
But that bargain basement luggage there
open on a bed of tangled sheets?
Mine? My lot to observe, not voyage,
voyeur in a bankrupt place.

Cold silence invests the streets.
Toward the sea ailing engines
thrust. Something more than boats
I have missed and lost
beyond possibility of recall.
The dark stern turns, home port erased,

turns under hills that hold fast
a nowhere town, secret
before tonight, and swallow
hull, deck, funnel, rigging, mast.
Furtively the wash caresses
the empty icons of a harbour

I may not depart,
even in my dreams.

Michael Baron

HOSPITALITY

No spit
Stitches out
Skin clipped
Strained muscles
Night nurse
Another fit
Doctors call
Can't sleep
Pain.
Eyes closed
Backward fall
Tubes attached
Lost hope
Life slips
Wheeled chairs
After care
Grey walls
Can't leave
Groans.
Curtains closed
Toilets locked
Sterile septic
Sickly smells
Moped floors
Stewed tea
In out
Emergency
Time slows
Last breath
Before death.

David Goldblatt

HALF A VOW

Prowling through the village of Albano
founded almost three thousand years ago
above Rome, sea slips, and the throaty queen
of post-modern Italian poetry
of pasta twirls and Milanese girls
(though she has forbidden me to shatter
the silence of her villa with keyclicks)
I am searching for nature's prostitute
(the other kind sitting on curbs, legs spread,
flicking tongues of high-pitched sound, heads around
like owls unafraid of blinders of night
smoking swarthy beauty away, are too
experienced (and expensive for I
have a promise to consummate with poor
class jingles) for all my inhibitions),
moon full of supersensuous yellows
surrounded by giant reds and white dwarfs,
willing to offer their light for my time,
astronomy back through astrology,
swift movement, their essential, for my space,
take from me as I am exposed, barter;
angle where the night cat forgives his prey,
turns furry head away from genital
to enjoy the catnip of anima.

Gross sexual assault on celibates
most often comes from clerics who do not
understand their own profession, believe
bodies almost good despite heretics
who boast they have never felt anything
or saints like Augustine who felt too much;
chastity without risk is half a vow.

Thomas Kretz

LONELINESS

Watching you sitting there, abstracted
By some thoughts hidden from me,
I know there's always a part of you
That will remain secret from me.
Your eyes shield themselves:
One-way mirrors of your soul. I
Love you totally and absolutely and
Without judgement. But where do I
Stand in your grand plan: Plain next
to your elegance, clumsy of thought,
Of word - you always aware,
Knowing what is right. You gave me
A beautiful child, so like her
Father, both leaving me behind.
But who could fail to love you?
And who could adore you more
Intently than I? What have I
Given you? Impatience and boredom
Often cross your face as you
Reflect upon something or someone
Else, far away from you.
Irritation masks your fine
Features and flickers in your
Deep eyes, leaving me friendless
And defeated: Wondering whether
To hurl myself at you in wanton
Abandonment, in a desperation only
I could feel - or withdraw,
Become reticent and discover or
Retrieve any remnants of self-respect
Or real independence. As I write
This I cry - too ashamed
For you to see - tears of self-pity?
Or tears which mourn a loss.
The loss of love. No longer sure
That I even fulfil a need,

Never mind part of your
Future or eternal destiny;
How can someone in my
Hapless body ever hope to
Sustain the wants and love
Of someone as special as you.

Ann McLeod

INTO ETERNITY

I noticed petals,
Petals gently falling;
Their perfume,
Wafted by a gentle breeze,
Seemed to stay,
As a dream
That goes on
Through mists of time;
The memory,
Lingering,
Yet drifting on,
And into eternity.

H V Horsfall

PUBLIC ADMINISTRATION

Lurking low in the village pool
the hungry crocodile hid the fool.

Poor fool, his life was only a trifle
and no-one bothered to lift a rifle -

till, to everyone's public grief,
the crocodile chose the local chief.

Thomas Land

BEHIND THE TILL

'£8.62 please.'

To you I am a hand in a glove,
Not someone to know
Nor someone to love.

I know your name,
You care not mine.
I give you the money:
Everything's fine!

Ten pound note into the till;
I smile at you yet still
You do not look up
Into my face.
Cash in the till
Its rightful place.

My hand outstretched
You give me my change . . .
'£1.38.'

My hand passes on.
Farewell my love.
It's not I that has gone
Only a glove.

It's another hand now
Older, more worn
With dirt caked nails
All tattered and torn.
It's repellent, it's gruesome,
Show it no love.
Remember me . . .

Remember My Glove.

David Wells

54

WASTED

His emaciated parents looked down
With pain-filled eyes at
His forlorn, rigid frame.
Dark skin, pale under the torrid midday sun
Luminous eyes curtained by
Fly-infested lids
Limbs and arms, grotesquely thin
A short, pain-wracked life
Not the untrammelled, carefree joy
Of a simplistic childhood.
Who was found wanting?

Edward Raymond Jones

KEY TO GOOD HEALTH

Acquire a certain amount of sleep
To avoid drowsiness which on one can creep
Exercise the body every day
To stay healthy along life's way.

Avoid tea, coffee, and pop containing caffeine,
And especially all forms of tobacco because of nicotine
Stay away from illegal drugs
And alcohol which will make the head buzz.

Eat fruit and veg every day
From milk and dairy products do not stray
Include meats, but use your head
Do not forget cereals and bread.

Brush your teeth, take daily baths and wear clean clothes
And when a cold occurs, don't forget to blow your nose.
See the dentist and doctor for regular check-ups
And take nine sips of water to cure the hiccups.

Molly Kathleen Thornton

ANNE BOLEYN

Still softly flows the Suir
Beside your birthplace out across the sea
You who denied a king his carnal lust
Till he had made you queen; and then you bore
Another queen but yet denied a son
The sun set on your fortunes and another
Was soon to take your place. You could not run
Back home to Carrick. Those who bore you ill
Prepared a headman's block on Tower Hill.

Roger Blackmore

THE TEENAGE DREAM

I really want to see you,
Though I know you never existed.
I want you to come and visit my room
Though I've become bitter and twisted.

I want this vision of my adolescence
To stand before my eyes,
And shower her with everything,
Beneath my darkened skies.

Christopher Keating

KALYPSO

You laugh a little now, Kalypso, but
your eyes are too big
and you take too long making up
your face become blank with
failure to be beautiful.
Just so

you paint your nails, just so
and pencil in new boundaries to your eyes.
The island weeps.
Your mirror's silver flakes
like sad confetti fall
each time you comb your hair.

David Alder

THE OUTCAST

The dark lady that walks the wards by night and whispers peace as
she glides by yellow candle light; my lady of the night;
The white starched linen cracks and bristles, as she bends over a
white pallor, that creakily, hangs on too life as best as can.
The incandescent gas mantle flickers and hisses as night drags on;
as pain ebbs and flows towards its conclusion peace.
The wheel turns and minds are bliss as yet another day is won,
as shafts of sun follow grey dawn rise.
Broken in body, but not in mind lies the penitent awaiting absolution
and its gift of pardon blest.
Words flow and letters wrote, that answers none, for the outcast,
beyond the family veil, as Black Sheep bleats across a cruel moor.
The spiritual metamorphosis gently works out the old hard practise,
by sweet words the Padre swings.
The seasons change and mark our route, as swinging down
the highway we went for many a good days end; never to rest upon a
good maids breast.
Cry shame on him that never did his best, but only for his
comfort cried; in his creed of God tolled down; that never
inheritance was blest for the touchstone of charity.
The Old Man near death, did seek holy Absolution for what he left,
as the Outcast stalks the mad wood for rest; till estate does pass the
shame will last, and crippled Nobility must pass.

J G Storey

ONWARD AND UPWARD

So many people out of work
Rising all the time!
Some they really like to shirk,
So they may have some perks!
It's no fun claiming benefits
When you realise that this is it
the lowest of low, the nearly down and out.
It's so sad to see so many about
Struggling to survive?
What a pittance, is there no hope?
It really makes you want to choke.
The barest minimum in what is allowed
enough, the law says! We aren't proud.
Change places for a few years
Our learned friends pin back your ears?
Times are changing o' so fast
It makes you wonder if we will be last.
Never fear our spirit is here
Put the great back in Britain
lead the world like we have done before
Our own backyard is more important.
Cutting costs, it's us that suffer
Can't have anything for supper.
Cutting costs is the all new thing
the government always out to sting
We will get over it and survive
We have to keep alive
Chin up and onward we must go
because we cannot afford to get so low.

Jim Strawbridge

SLIPPING

Slipping the rope
taut
over ankle

I watched him
flinching
like a wet fish
slowly drying

slapping his applause
on the deck

pillows of plastic
pulsating
watching for the
encore

sure of the evening press.

K P McIntyre

THE METEOR

In a prison
A ball of fire flashes like lightning
And falls in a marsh
Like a stone
And the prisoners
All splashed with the mud
For a little instant
Shine
Radiant with joy
There must be somebody
Who still remembers me
And my existence frittered away
There is still some hope for me today

Angela Matheson

THE RECOVERY

It's getting better now
The pain, though there, is not as constant, comes and goes,
Like grief it washes over me when least expected,
And leaves me half drowned upon the shore,
Then warmed by the sunshine of kindness of a dear friend
I drag myself back to some semblance of normality
And face another day.

My battered self esteem lies bruised as a muggers victim in the
gutter,
Yet now and then a word, an action, from someone uninvolved
Lifts my heart, my hopes, and says that there is more,
Another life awaits if only I can ride the storm of my emotions and
Find the strength in self belief and optimism.

Perhaps I will look back one day and see how strong I was,
To find the courage which I now must summon.
To make perhaps the most important choice I'll ever make,
To live my life for me and save my self respect and sanity.

Jill Frances Stephenson

MY GRANDFATHER'S SHED

My grandfather's shed
Smelt of pinewood and cedar,
Rosin and polish,
Cigars and damp string.

In its dark depths he pottered,
Repotted and woodworked
Through the short days of winter
And on into spring.

On bright summer mornings
He sat in the doorway
And blinked his pale eyes
Like a mole in the light.

Then in autumn he gathered
The fruits of the garden
And stored them away
In the shed, out of sight.

His shed was his home,
His refuge and cloister.
In its confines his schemes
And his dreams, all were born.

Now he's gone and I'm here,
Sorting nails from old wire,
In his shed, the one place
Where it seems right to mourn.

Tracy Atkinson

SUFFOLK

Reprinted from *Poems For Us All by Paul Volante*

Suffolk, oh! Suffolk, what have they done
Your buildings of fine art all tattered and torn apart
Landscape of beauty and colour
Surrounded with broken glass everywhere you pass
Towns, villages and parks all have their marks
Plastic and paper link our Suffolk hearts
From land to sea, there is no room for you and me
Only the beauty of the rubbish suffocating me
Would it be too much to ask not to let Suffolk slide on it's arse
This junk you scatter over Suffolk's county
Belongs in the bin - or should we jump therein
Cans and discarded cars have all left their scars
Oh! Suffolk, a county of rare beauty and people of duty
Wake up! Before it's too late and don't be like your mate
That leaves his junk inside Suffolk's gate . . .

Paul Volante

THE FAIR

Dying silhouettes tango in the sugary light,
Through candy clouds and ice-cream,
Waltzing waves drool foam onto the frosted sand,
Honeycombed sun melts to another generation.
A snake of exhilaration observes the peace
After the strenuous hours of treacled toddlers,
Fudge fortresses and caramel castles.
Dizzy horses snooze in the stillness,
Outsize wheel creaks with relief as its hinges relax
And the buckets swing freely,
The deserted bingo hall revels in the silence,
Distorting mirrors reflect only themselves,
And the chocolate stains printed by tiny hands of innocence.
Grateful coconuts lie in their beds,
Butterscotch trickles decorate the days laughter,
Gutters ooze with toffee licks.
The moons silver rays stroke the concrete,
Massaging away the day's trials
Until morning mists tickles the world,
And wakes the sticky sleep.

Claire Chilcott

UBIQUITOUS BROWN PAPER

Keeping your clothes clean from the Chinese laundry,
a rustling guard against the dirt and dust of Yanji.

Bribing the key ministers of far-off ministries,
a crinkled shield for a government's lack of integrity.

Wrapping the birthday present to post to your nipper,
a sello-taped buffer for the ride of a postal tripper.

Ironing your trousers or pressing that pleat,
an opaque mask that screens from the heat.

Transporting your meal from the *Taj* Indian take-away,
a crackling veil, over tinfoil, keeps the cold at bay.

Disguising porno magazines that display lacy lingerie,
a wrinkled cloak for your lack of maturity.

Holding nuts, bolts and screws, your Sunday's DIY,
a fluttering cover keeps the prize from a prying eye.

Plugging the gaping hole in a smashed window pane,
shutting out the draught, but not keeping Him out again.

Bringing books from the shop to satisfy your yearning,
a neatly folded shroud to hold in the learning.

A glue-sniffer's inhaler for a car-park's stolen moments,
soaked with a trip of psycho-corrosive solvents.

Ornette Coltrane

CONFESSIONS

When he was taken to the flat
he knew he was done for
three days of beatings
submersions
taped confessions.

Then he was driven over the border
so others there
could have a piece of the meat
he was stripped
to his underwear
shot twice in the head
his body booby-trapped
and left
at the side of an isolated road.

Gary Allen

HEAVEN?

I soon learned to fix, ain't lived till now
The powder pours through my body
pulsating in my head
a cataract of sensation.
Night and day fall into the bright sun
I experience fire's heat and ice cold.
My eyes search the heights, I'm afraid
of the dark abyss that creeps around
the spectacular glory of whirling colours,
I must see light, I don't want my soul
to leak away in shadows.
Scag is a miracle; no pain, no
confusion. I have found heaven.
Haven't I?

Eileen Fairclough

REVELATION (UP-DATE)

Apocalypse is on us now, it seems,
As rank Materialism rules the day,
And Mammon leads the masses Satan's way
Towards the vacuous vortex of their dreams;
So Armageddon is redundant now,
For selfishness and greed dictate the play
And soulless cynicism has its say,
While murky media tells us Why, and How!

The innocence is dead, the glory spent,
The Godhead guillotined, and gone away,
The many-headed monster's here to stay
With fangs sunk deep in sick Society:-
The Day is almost done, and I must weep
For all the small, sad sighing of Humanity.

Dick Hedger

IF I HAD ALL THE POWER ON EARTH

If I had all the power on earth
I would use it very well
I would feed the poor and destitute
and help them all I could.
I would make showers of rain
come down at night
on dry and arid land
I would make crops grow
Where no crops grow
and the rivers to run free.

If I had all the power on earth
I would know just what to do
I would share out all the wealth there is
and give everyone his due.
There would be no rich or poor
no high or low
and no mighty millionaires
I would make this world a paradise
for everyone to share.

If I had all the power on earth
I would be busy all the time
I would round up all the wicked ones
and send them down the mines.
I would make them work day and night
to purify their souls
I would cast a spell on all of them
and turn them into toads.

If I had all the power on earth
I would be very tired by now
I would be loved by some
of the multitudes
and disliked by more than a few
I would book myself a holiday
and hand over the power to you.
Barbara Geraghty

ARMISTICE

The eleventh hour
The eleventh day
The eleventh month

Remember.

A delicate canopy,
Scarlet flowers suspended
Above boundless years.
Perfumed petals poignant in their intimacy.

Remember.

Waves of blood soaked blooms
Ripple across the conflict years.
Crimson shrouds
Over weeping graves.

Remember.

Black death chokes;
White pain sears;
Grey despair seeps.
All hope wanes.

Remember.

Broken bodies lie;
Callow life wastes;
The heart's blood spills,
Tomorrow's future fades.

Remember.

Forever will there be
A canopy of blood red poppies,
Overlaying man's intolerance
To colour, creed, blood, belief.

Remember.

The eleventh hour
The eleventh day
The eleventh month.

Remember.

Barbara Scarfe

THE STOKER

Body damp and soiled
This lackey born to serve
And feed a furnace.
Its insatiable maw
Ever seeking more and more
From this his shovel.
Searching for the
Power of steam.

He stops at six . . .
. . . his pause is earned,
This is when his effort shows
How, if correctly placed,
Each shovelful of coal
Will feed the flames to keep the pressure high,
As shown upon the gauge which measures
Power of steam.

'Six at a time' is what his tutors said.
Six at a time to make the fire glow.
It's red that makes the steam to blow
The pistons back and forth at speed.
A flame will make a deal of smoke,
But smoke will never satisfy an engine's need,
Nor yet produce the
Power of steam.

Gordon Litchfield

THINGS LEFT UNSAID

You seem so old now,
Bird claw hands,
Aspiration reaching out no further than flesh.
But I leave all that clean, disjointed,
Like things left unsaid for others to hear.

You said once when you were a young girl,
You raced along the top of the high stonewalls
near the farmhouse,
Right out to the railway lines and back . . .
Seemed as though you had simply held the scent
Of a single moment within you all your life . . .

Just lately I've thought of a swing
Across a stretch of water,
Where kids with fifty pence nets
Still catch sticklebacks on warm August afternoons.
I dragged most of my innocence
through those local summers.
Told this place things I dared not even say to myself.
Sometimes it seems as though
The windows of this room might burst,
With warm fields and sheetmetal roads,
Like giant drops of saltwater
Clinging to a child's naked spine.

I wonder what makes life so precise, pretty,
And full of so much longing.
Like these filthy council house roofs,
As they dip into another morning's sun.

P A Stone

SCAPEGOATS

Those goats which Aaron took
for the Jews' atonement had
an even chance to win
in the Almighty's book.
Nowadays, mum and dad
are certs to bear the sin.

'We are the future, those
for whom no lots were cast.
We have no cause for shame:
every historian knows
the present is made by the past.
We should not take the blame!'

From ravaged Edens come
the cries of innocence:
'The fault's not ours but others'
In parliament and home
they destroy the evidence
and martyr fathers and mothers.

Those in trouble must find
one who is culpable:
a soldier for war, the old
for being both old and blind,
the careful for what they cull,
the rich for having gold.

One generation perhaps
atoned with an evens bet
which lost. That fated corps
of ordinary chaps
settled their monstrous debt
by dying in the First World War.

J R Holt

HOUSE CLEARANCE

Amongst these last, improbable things
that rattle in the bottom of their wardrobe,
a long forgotten, yet unmistakable, object
that speaks more eloquently than all else
of childhood moments lingering in the
reassuring ambit of bedroomly, parental indulgence.

A large, octagonal bottle which used,
in those days of infant wonder, to sit upon
an embroidered runner, as if accorded
a special place that only grown-ups understood.
Within, a green, aromatic water
that never failed a simple, olfactory sampling.

Now empty, forlorn, yet deeply resonant.
Just one twist of its chromium-plated,
spherical stopper may, even now, underwrite
those mysteries and memories of the
nineteen-thirties. Twist, flick and spin.
A last, improbable trace of scented water

sweetens the intervening years with Eau-de-Cologne.

John Fineran

I AM COMMODITY

I am commodity, I am for sale
Look - see how cheap I am!
I am used and exploited, I am bought and sold
I will sell myself to anyone, I have no choice

I am commodity, this brain's for hire
Feed me and clothe me and keep me warm
Allow me some rest from time to time
I will last a lifetime - guaranteed

70

I walk and talk and work hard for you
I say what you want, I do what you say
I do anything to please you. All the time I hate you
Can't live with you, can't survive without you

But beware, beware fat cat
For there are those, not unlike myself
Who say the time will come when the hate will overflow
The frustration and despair will swell up and burst, over you fat cat
And I think they are right
And it won't be too long
And you will be dead
And I will be free, not commodity.

Dave Stockley

THE POET'S NIGHTMARE

There is nothing quite so daunting
As a piece of paper flaunting . . .
Go on . . . fill me . . . go on . . . fill me
Go on . . . fill me . . . if you can.

For that piece of paper lying
On the desk of there defying
Bring a thankless kind of blankness
But no answers on demand!

Now go to bed and try a'dreaming
And the mind will start a'scheming
To get you to your pen again
Before the freezing break of dawn.

But, get you up and jot the gist
Of the stanzas nearly missed
Then the battle with the papyrus
Will bring surrender...in the morn.

Ted Herbert

STATIONARY WORDS

Here we stand
Train at hand
In silence
Platform staring
Words withdrawing
Words deserting
Words with inconsequential
Meaning
Words at sea
Searching for land
Words running out
Like hour-glass sand
Timetabled words
Rigid and bland
Left on a platform station.

John J Parry

THE DESERT DREAM

They speak of dreams, that once were real.
  A bath. A drink. A girl. A meal.
But I dream of a bed, with blankets and things.
  A mattress and pillow. A mattress with springs.
With soft cotton sheets, to caress my burnt skin
  And no desert fleas, to find their way in.
Air that is cool. No burning heat
  Or sand in the bed. No stinking feet.
With silent guns, that wouldn't bark
  That I could sleep, when it is dark.
And no blind fool, just over the way
  Playing at God, turning night into day.
In search of a hole, where I hide in fright
  And dream of a bed, to sleep at night.

Ron Ellis

72

DEATH - FEAR - HIM

I felt it today
Following me through the rain
Smelt the grim stench,
Almost endured the pain,
Closer and closer,
Experiencing heat,
- hearing *pitter-patter*
Of nature's heartbeat.

Death

I've dreamt of his footsteps,
Know of the sound,
Today the dark shadow
Decaying all-round,
I finally understood
Of the victims hell claim,
Their achilles is fear
To feed is his aim.

Fear

As our hearts beat,
Our pulses race,
When the muscles spasm,
Death takes his place,
When we panic at pain -
Feel mortality hear,
A hole in the soul
Is created by fear.

Him

He crawls inside,
And taking control,
There's no place to hide
When he dines
On your Soul ...

Sarah Grant

THE SQUARE PEG

"Not my scene, " with a nervous titter,
"Parties, I mean," he said,
"For the heat, the racket and glitter
Give me pain in my mind and my head.

Talking rubbish and talking it loudly
To people who don't want to hear,
With an air of what is avowedly
Artificial bonhomie and cheer.

Committees and business and politics
Equally, leave me quite cold.
I can't concentrate on these antics
And my spirit can't seem to take hold.

In the midst of an earnest discussion
As I doodle around all the blots
I am ravished by the notes of a thrush on
A twig on the dancing tree-tops.

Not my scene, all the washing and pushchairs,
Of suburban family life:
Supermart, telly and fish-shop,
And cosy, incestuous strife.

And yet - not my scene either,
Pale cloister and quiet cell,
The glimmering flame on the altar:
They attract me - but also repel."

But moonlight and dappled water
Or bright notes from a wandering bird,
Cleaved his heart between tears and laughter
As if voices of angels he'd heard.

Dreamy-eyed, in his garden he'd wander,
Not to dig, though he carried a spade:
Not to plant, but with wondering finger
Touching petal, and leaf, and green blade.

Maybe his true scene had no actors,
All his life he had read the wrong plays:
Soliloquies would have been apter
For him. On his own. All his days.

Maggy Parsons

STILL LAUGHING ALL THE WAY TO THE RIVER BED

It's been a pleasant night.
You and your friends
have ways of making me laugh.
Good company,
young,
vibrant and young,
I take my leave, finally.
Finally take my leave
still laughing,
laughing,
still laughing
  all the
    way to the
      bar room door.

Good company,
young,
vibrant and young,
I take my dive, finally.
Finally take my dive
still laughing,
laughing,
still laughing
  all the
    way to the
      river bed.

Darren Peers

ROWAN'S HAT

Rowan's hat is not on the sideboard now,
It is bobbing along the sidewalks of New York
And strolling with her down Fifth Avenue.
If you watch the Easter Parade
You will see it stark among the floppy violets
And the straw extravagances
Like a black pudding at a Lord Mayor's banquet.
She will wear it as she eats up the city
And spits out the pips;
She will build her First Collection round it,
And, unless you wear a Rowan,
No-one will invite you to a Washington party
And you could die disgraced;
Sitting on the back of the open limmo
In the ticker-tape parade
She will wave it in triumph at the cheering crowds;
And brushed and retextured it will appear
At Buck House to be made a Dame with her
For services to British Fashion.
Look for them both on the famous balcony
Where they will join the suitably hatted Royals
For the R.A.F. fly past in Black Pudding formation.

While awaiting its victorious return
I am ordering a glass case
And making a golden-tasselled purple velvet cushion
For its permanent display;
The sideboard is daily dusted and waxed weekly
As I fully expect the V. and A. to request it
For the Rowan Exhibition which will rock the world!

Mary Mestecky

TAO TE CHING

A moon drop
falls
into the pond
of night
sending its ripples
in ever
widening
Circles
through
the Cosmos.

Stephen Gyles

THE GIVING

A mind's closet
opened wide
revealed expanse
no where to hide

shifting sand
becoming rock
all loose ends
tied as thought

self-expression
struggling free
laying bare
a faith to see

and from this
taking heart
the individual
gives us art

Don Ammons

EMPLOYMENT TRAINING '90

I was sitting in the glasshouse,
Gawping at my screen
Surrounded by the 'past-it' swots,
Well you know what I mean,
They were varied from black to white,
(We like to patronise),
But all had muddled confused brains
Behind their glassy eyes,
The teacher wandered round and round
(And rather round she be)
As time wore on and life passed by
Into eternity,
Outside a war was being fought
With people being killed,
But the only true threat to us
Was our not being skilled,
I got pissed off just sitting there
And started writing verse,
But as I got right into it
It started getting worse,
Eventually I got so bored,
It would not go away,
Hoping the enemy would drop
Their bombs on us today,
I thought our boys were brave as they
Put their lives on the line,
But they are really living more
Than us and doing fine,
For unlike us they are well paid
Enjoying themselves too
While all we do is wish we had
Things we could spend and do,

And so it goes, we just drag on
Gawping at our screens,
Bereft of hope, spiritually dead,
Living beyond our means.

Abey

GRADUATION DAY

Parents arrive;
Their voices hum like bees
Outside a hive,
Sweetened by degrees.
Old and young,
On this auspicious day,
Are all at one.

In they throng!
With pearl grey lounge suits;
The odd sarong:
The wide brimmed summer hats,
By ladies worn:
Cameras by the gents
All bravely borne.

The graduates!
Adorned as learning's brides;
Now radiate
Youthful triumph and pride:
Hold their degree:
All barriers now passed;
Eager and free.

Proud parents pose;
Sharing their daughter's day:
She, blushing like a rose
With her M.A.

Alexander K Sampson

JUSTICE FOR THE INNOCENT VICTIMS, WHERE IS IT?

Lying crumpled in a corner, lifeless and still, the slaughter of an
innocent child has taken a final fall. The Men of Law shouting at the
door, too late, they only hear the last gasp of life's unanswered call
         "Come ahead you mugs!"
Twist and turns of bloodstained handcuffs, the calculated flow of
crocodile tears. "You'se don't understand, I loved her as my own, I
couldn't help it, it was the Drugs!" Substitute parent goes kicking and
fighting all the way from this death soaked filled room. Hardened
Police Officers weep silently inside, years of specialist Training helps
hide their dismal gloom. An Officer takes a single lily from a nearby
vase, lays it gently beside this innocent child, her life abruptly ended,
lying alone shattered and broken "Goodbye Sweet Tiger Lily, a gift
from The Boys in Blue, a small but heartfelt farewell token"
Ten months later the New Lord Olivier gives his greatest
performance during his 5 year stay in the Prison Yard to his 'captive
audience' The Big Man wholly swaggers, other prisoners glare at
him, knife him with their rage filled eyes, like ice cold Daggers. "Look
at me, remorse I show you'se all, its here for all to see, carved in my
face!" Yeah Pal, you fooled the Jury, you can't fool them, they know
what exactly you are thinking, the truth behind your charade.
"Your all mugs, its that little Bastards fault I'm in here in the first
place!"

Charles Murphy

GRANDMA

My memory is one - at 7 years of age
A gentle sweet face, aged and worn
The photos are few, faded and old
She lives in me, but I don't know where!

I look like her so they all say
But do I think like her?
Do I feel like her?
She lives in me, but I don't know where!

What was she like when young?
Shy like me, timid and quiet?
Did she walk like me, talk like me?
She lives in me but I don't know where!

Were her dreams of youth
Full of hope like mine?
Did she yearn for ideals?
She lives in me but I don't know where!

Did she meet trouble head on?
Her feet on the ground
A spine of steel and a spirit of faith
She lives in me but I don't know where!

In middle age, content and serene
Fashioned by life - too late to change
I wonder what might have been!
She helped me here but I don't know from where!

One day in the future we'll meet
Two strangers face to face
We'll talk and I'll learn
Just where she lived in me!

Louise C Evans

ROOTS

You did not hoe
You did not know
In planting days ago.
That as your own
Time period grows old
Desire comes aglow.
Now that you know
It's too late to sow.

Ronald Simpson

THE VANITY OF MAN (THE VAIN MAN)

His gaze transfixed upon himself,
  A hero he doth see;
A knight, a warrior, a saint;
  Perhaps! he sees all three.

His vision, blinkered by his plight,
  Does not see those in need;
And adoration's his sole right;
  Yes! vanity's his creed.

Paolo De Grazio

A PLEA FOR SILENCE

Let me turn
From the sound of people
to the voice of the river.
Here on the bank
I hear its quiet words
rippling towards me
over the stones
needing no answer.

Let me turn
from human speech
to the voice of the trees,
standing silently together
in the water meadows
until the wind
stirs the leaves
to a whisper.

Let me turn
from clattering tongues
to the dry stone walls
that are speechless.

Deirdre Armes Smith

IPSO FACTO

Existence is. Sad but true. I think. I am.
A Buddhist on an island off the Scottish coast,
shaven and tattooed, in robes of rust and gold,
calmly grubs a lean subsistence from the dirt
beneath his blistered feet. His quiddity,
that which makes him what he is,
his captious subtlety, his being, is illusive.
Existence and desire walk hand in hand
in sober truth on the shores of the sea,
brother and sister, stubborn in the will to crush
the warm stirring of old habits. Grounded,
their sandalled footprints light upon the pale sand,
cool under the sun, soothed by the bell
and the prayer bowl, let sense prevail
on wanton sensuality, base hunger,
need, voracity, devotion, longing, lust.
Existence is. Sweet and sad. I want therefore I am.

Tessa Bailey

PRAGUE SPRING

He would remember
Monday afternoon along the banks of the Vltava
always
in the city that had learnt to whisper
the idle chattering strokes
of boats on the river
mingled with the music
drifting unfettered from the Charles Bridge
where 21 saints stand guard
blindfolds of that August lost
but still mute
to tell what they never did see.

Richard Clarke

83

ODE TO JIMMY BOYLE (THE GLASGOW EX-GANGSTER)

There was a wild Glaswegian boy
His name was Jimmy Boyle
He grew up in the Gorbals
Where life's all strife and toil
Where drunken fights are daily scenes
And every word's a curse
For bringing up a child it's hard
To find a place that's worse.

His father died when he was just
a lad of barely five
His mother worked three jobs a day
Just so they could survive
And Jimmy roamed the Gorbals streets
With mud and rats his toys
They made their fun with what they could
Those poor, deprived wee boys

Survival of the fittest
was the motto of the place
To be rough and tough and violent
Was the way to keep up face
So he became a man too soon -
No time to be a child
The leader of a gang, he was
Notorious and wild
To the criminals of Glasgow town
He was a man of fame
And people used to tremble
At the mention of his name

Then came the day he had to pay
for the bad that he had done
He was sentenced to a life in jail
for many years to come
He was brutalised and victimised -
Deprived of all his pride
But the violence he'd seen out there
Was just the same inside
They took away his human rights
They took away his shame
But his strong and fighting spirit
Was the thing they couldn't tame

Man's inhumanity to man
Has long been recognised
But sometimes a spark of decency
Can therein be disguised
The phoenix builds his funeral pyre
and then himself cremates
And out of his own ashes
He again himself creates

So Jimmy Boyle, his spirit free
Arose from all the mire
The dormant good inside of him
Awakened to inspire -
The thinker and the artist
Who'd been hidden deep within
He showed that there was more to him
Than flesh and bone and skin
There still are many folk who
When they hear his name, recoil
But with pride someday
His son may say,
Ma dad was Jimmy Boyle.

Marina Saleem

SPEAKING FOR A FRIEND

I spoke for thee old friend
Today I spoke for thee
So that at the end
They too could see.
Oh! they all knew about
The booze, the chat, the women,
But what you did and were
Did not occur.

They looked at me
And I could see
The depreciating smiles
Both sides of the aisle,
Which did and didn't ask me -
To speak for thee,
Not just perhaps, because
We were companions boon.
Or that I'd follow soon!

I gazed upon the Union Flag
Which covered you
I hope you heard me?
A few minutes in the hour
Is I know for any - quite enough
But yet, was all too little
To say all I might of you.
Those verbal fights
Those comradely, dangerous,
Called-out long nights.

The ideal civvy-street hopes
We had; and flying kites, mostly
For what we thought was right
Now all we fought for negated
In Ideology warring on its own.

To think - we thought we'd won ! -
I wore a Poppy - it was White,
So much obscured or out of sight.
All heard the Bugle's peal
(They sent a Drummer up from Deal).

It does not matter,
That none heard me too
Standing silent in my pew
But Oh! it did matter
That I spoke for you.

Jack Lacey

ZEUS

A thin black wedge from where I am standing:
a sky-beast pondering his cruel landing.
The fields stop their shaking, waiting, waiting,
whilst he stands on the breeze, floating, floating.
They say "Bring him his prize, bring him his prize!"
They say "Satiate the God of the Skies!"
Who will be the victim forced from his den,
thrust with a wild scream into the open?
The creatures peep out in dry-mouth terror;
to withhold a catch? - a foolish error!
They say, "Find him, for this Zeus cannot wait,
before his patience transforms to unbridled hate.
For to the sun he will turn his red eye
and on scorched earth we will be forced to lie;
no water and we will all die of thirst,
and all this for a coward? Let him be cursed!"

A mother, yelping, pushes forth her son -
innocent, helpless - the swooping is done.
Her nest is still full, but one is far off,
the one forced to placate the Sky-God's wrath.

Peter Harris

PROGRESS?

It's called *"progress"* the young all try to tell me
All change is improvement, it all has to be.
I try to explain change is not always best
Do we have to accept bad along with the rest?

Villages of beauty disappearing fast are
To make speedier ways for the Wonder God 'Car'.
It's speed that kills, we're told eighty a day!
Now come to your senses all youngsters I pray.

Don't rush so fast that you will pass by
Many a sight to gladden the eye.
An old thatched roof, an old fashioned bower
Of old cottage plants, all out in full flower.

Do stop and let gladden the other sense, Nose
The sweet smell of Pinks, Honeysuckle and Rose.
But I waste my words, past all they do scurry
'Mid exhaust fumes, all in such a great hurry.

No time to exchange a smile and a chat
As in days of yore, of this and of that.
Oh why are they always in such a great haste,
Is it improvement? Or is it just waste?

Rushing here and there and hither and yon
Arrived too early? Then switch Telly on.
They sit and they stare with mouths all agape
This is called *Progress!* - Or is it just Fate?

Gwen Mason

THE TIME IS OUT OF JOINT

Did Shakespeare feel the deepening spiral of despair
When pen to paper bore poetic fruit?
No reason soothes my aching "Why?", " What can I do?".
'Twas reason brought me here . . .
How could it bear me hence?
And anyway, just where is hence?
Can't say I'd want to go, -
Especially with him.
Reason is no friend of mine.
My friend, myself, I fear is gone from me . . .
So long dismissed, unworthy . . .
Yet small, and far, I almost hear the whisper
Of a once forgotten line.
A simple . . . thoughtful phrase so well transports my soul
To a safe and gentler space.
The time is out of joint
And nothing more

Janet Foster McKee

A LONELY VIEW ON A BUSY DAY

Eternal imperfections of the mortal.
An incessant din of inability;
A piercing scream of vulernability.
The scornful eye cast on others
Yet blindness to see within.

Hearing a distance call
I am swept under a wave of hypocrisy,
The tide of criticism ebbing on
As life flounders and fails.

I walk on, facing the wind,
Feeling the freedom,
Mockingly joyful of my loneliness in the crowd.

Chris J Ducker

AT 3am

the clock is ticking solid death.
a melancholy car horn hoots, far off.
the drunks vomit truth in the subways.
the moon looks tubercular and catholic
at 3am.
security guards walk empty offices
trying to feel alive.
dogs bark across gardens.
you in your dreams hedge-hopping.
young in your dreams, old in your bed
at 3am.
somewhere an insomniac poet
wrestles with his rhymes . . .
clover . . . dover . . . pullover
and crosses out his cliches
with a burning biro.
the night stirs a froth of stars
and cracked saxophones in sleeping ears
where the ocean roars
drips
pounds
on doors
and dogs' dreams.

at 3am
a child is beaten.

at 3am
night-buses thread through dreaming suburbs
where murderers sleep innocent sleep,
housewives sleep tidy sleep,
and hangmen;
the deepest sleep.

at 3am
monuments stand unobserved.
perhaps they relax,
the mounted dismount
soldiers charging into battle
halt. chat.
and the night
blistered and peeled
in your skull
in the grave
runs
flows
a night impenetrable
a night unknowable
at 3am.

and at 3am
you arise
swallow aspirin
and wonder if this night
this 3am
will ever end.

Martin Vega

BEDSIT TOILET SONG

If you're scared of spiders
I'd advise ya,
don't close the door,
'cos I found out before
I aint no arachnid assassin,
and this is a bloody small space
to have a panic attack in.

Sarah Hughes

SLAVE TO THE NIGHT

Daylight subsides -
Taking Her claim of all that is rational and real.
Leaving darkness, Her greatest adversary,
free to play with my imagination and memory.

The darkness possesses me -
Conquering my body and soul.
He is all powerful, while I am as small as a mouse,
existing purely for His pleasure.

He promises me happiness,
bribes me into worshipping Him,
then laughs at me as He makes the happiness fade
into the surrounding solitude.

He torments me but there is no escape.
I am a subject in His Kingdom of the Night,
unable to release the chains with which He binds me.
He is my Master and I have no choice but to obey.

His tyranny is suppressed when Daylight returns,
She takes me under Her wing, soothing me into reverie.
Daylight is the epitome of all that is beautiful,
but She cannot compete with Darkness,
and once again He takes control of me
and I become a Slave to the Night.

Susan Gifford

WHEN YEARS HAVE FLOWN

At ease I glimpse TV
to screen a man I think is old
and pity him his age.
One other actor speaks: "Your age just 53"
so I am shocked same age as me
where did the years go to?

I challenge man in mirror
who gave you shadow beneath your eyes
who painted your hair grey?
which make-up artist lends you wisdom
affected to the end
where did the years go to?

Who issued pain to rear
to tell of times too arduous;
O if when young had taken care -
who hid away the rules?

The young now older:- is some sign
they find it grim to realise
how the years have flown . . .

Herbert Wilson

TRINITY CENTENARY

One hundred years of history
Lie within church walls
Spire pointing like a finger - skyward, tall.

It has outlived five monarchs
And three cruel wars.
Not as a fortress - but with open doors.

It has housed precious moments,
Many joys and tears.
Has sacrificed its sons - in sadder years.

One hundred years of history
And then one hundred more.
Take courage for the future.
Hopes, like spires, must upward soar.

Jean Wolff

POETRY

What is poetry?
Is it the lilting writing of an educated hand?
Or the passion flamed mind seeking expression?

Not for me, the pretty waters so calm,
But like a torrent, tumbling and roaring,
My spirit must have rein to soar,
to touch the skies, and plunge the depths into despair,
Love, hate, envy, need and compassion are the
essential composites of poetry that matters,
Loneliness, happiness and fulfilment add
their spice to the magic brew.

But how can poetry exist without heart and passion?
It is like weak tea, or flat and featureless as a great plain.
Talking pretty words, soon bores those who
would listen, *but*, if you feel your poetry
you will inspire those who listen, they will
feel moved, as they recognise emotions
within themselves.

The powerful words of the long-dead still inspire
and are enjoyed by the hungry minds
of those who seek to learn.

In poetry every generation can add its own contribution
to the colourful fabric and tapestry,
that is poetry. Ad Infinitum.

John C Hibbert

SINGLE BEDS (FOR JENNY)

Sometimes I'd lie there, listening
As you prised yourself asleep.
Never easy, the sleeping together;
The bed too small, unleavened,
No inch of it quite home.

And that elbow-sharp digging
Of your other's silence,
The unreadable Braille
Of what was really thought.
Hard, placing one's sleep in trust.

Awake, the fears stack and circle,
Doubts about the being there
And about the being gone.
You sleep on, each breath a space bar,
Your limpness like a steel.

Until, with the crying of Louise,
Rise sudden, naked, luminous,
And fold without a passing glance
Into the only bed you need.
That love, at least, DNA encoded.

Martyn John Lowery

THE SAME CAN MAKE A DIFFERENCE

In the garden
Damp air
Hung around her washing,
Refusing to dry.

In the lounge
A sluggish vacuum
Was bounced over her wool-mix,
Declining to clean.

She had hung out her washing.
She had vacuumed the floor.
The drying was immaterial.
The cleaning didn't count.
Just going through the motions
Kept the blackness out.

Carol Ann Frodsham

TRAMPS

'every Person wandering abroad and lodging in any barn or
outhouse, or any deserted or unoccupied building, or in
the open air, or under a tent, or in any cart or wagon, not
having any visible means of subsistence, and not giving a
good account of himself or herself . . .'

Vagrancy Act 1824

'They are there tonight and they will be there tomorrow night . . .
the thousands of people, who, when most of us are in our beds,
are out there sleeping rough in derelict buildings, barns,
hedgerows, under the sky; wrapped in newspapers, old sacks,
old clothes.'

Jeremy Sandford
Down and Out in Britain (1971)

Last night where I slept only the stars observed
My dreaming body beaten up by the skinhead cold
And assaulted by gangs of wind and rain. Sold
For sixpence my town gear soaked when cars swerved

Thudding thunder through the darkening tunnel of my head
As I arose to shake myself free of the filth. Now
Staggering skywards from the dungy ditch of my bed
I stumble through city slush, remembering the warmth of snow.

As I lay there with the wild flakes whirling around
Like a million mad moths I thought of Christmases ago
And the first one especially. Like a mole underground
I emerged from the freezing dark to recollect how

It was once then. Yes, swirling masses of strangers
Parading indifference past me, I was like you too.
The world flowed to me through artificial filters.
Now I raise myself like a wildflower to greet you.

Through strangling smogs I saw where the sky is blue.

In Paris on the Left Bank I met him along the Pont Neuf.
His muddy jacket and ragged trousers stretched
Like scarecrows around the muscular machine of his body.
With clawing nails the night wind scratched
Terrible torments driving him to me.

Roland Gurney

VIOLET WEEDS

The brush of darkened trees
Make a beacon of the sun
Oblivious to yesteryears inscription
She waits for nothing
Lost in reminiscence
She sits as a broken animal
Upon the old grey tombstone
Her eyes follow the violet weeds
All along the road which lead
To a beautiful kind of shame
To those under earth
Now swimming in starlight
Fading in pictures past
Decaying in magnetic structures
Lost in video tapes
Lost in life
Honey sweet melancholy
Enshrouds her
In the sensuous clothing
Of the dead
As a finger traces a crack
Across the moss diseased monument
And for three complete seconds
She forgets what she is.

Val Denham

CATS, COTTAGES AND CARE

Cats cradles, cats!
Thatched cottages and gardens,
Music and Milton.
These conjure up cosy, country thoughts.
A ticking clock upon a mantle shelf.
Peaceful, sunny afternoons,
Amidst butterflies and the hum of bees.
In Hertfordshire.
Beside streams where wild foxgloves grow
And poppies bob their pert red caps.
Snowdrops and primroses beneath yet to be.
You walking beside me.
The cat curled up beside the hearth.
The woodfire burning in the grate.
The witches broom upon the wall
The herbal smells.
Sweet briar.
Crumpets toasted for tea.
All thoughts which are dear to me.
The new born babe suckling in its mother's arms,
An abundant woman with ample breasts.
Roast chestnuts roasting by the fire.
The smile upon your face,
The happy smile of one who knows true love and
how to make it grow.
A brass band in a village park.
A dew kissed red rose picked just for me.
These are the thoughts which kindle my heart and last
through all eternity.

Elma Melvin

CARBOOTING

I'm in the queue,
Crushed and pushed,
Hemmed in by the punters.

In at last,
What to see,
Every stall is crowded.

Push to the front,
What the hell,
Or miss out on the bargains.

Just my luck
Wrong kind of stuff
Battle back out again.

The old and the new,
Displayed to view,
Measure the passage of time.

I reach out my hand,
Oh! not again,
Someone has beaten me to it.

I've done the round,
Enjoyed the crowd,
Picked up two very nice vases.

Home at last,
Nice cup of tea,
Feet up very relaxing.

But take my advice,
Be first in the queue,
If ever you take up carbooting.

M Hunter

THE MAVERICK

I smooth the soft, silky warmth of
her fur, and feel the hooked claws
treading in ecstasy on my knee.

A minute ago she was crawling
through undergrowth and now,
appetite sated, is stretched
luxuriously in front of the fire.

I stroke the bony head and cradle
her yielding flesh in my arms,
rewarded by her responsive purr.

Dot Martin

UNTITLED

Unbound, her hair hangs like nooses,
She is suspended unemotion,
Rapt in cloistered silence.

In the hollow hours,
Between dusk and dawn,
She stalks my starling heart,
Feline,
Unseen,
But whispering of love,
And the lies of God.

Robert Southern

NIGHT THOUGHTS

Dad: the thud of a corpse hitting the floor.
Dad: a stain in my flesh irremovable.
Dad: a sound without love.
Dad: a word with no name.

Tara King

THE CHURCH SPIRE

From the jumble of houses
Across the tarmac
Beyond the rough ground,
A finger on the skyline
Pointing cloudwards,
Basking in golden light
That flows its length,
The neighbourhood awash in
Its glow,
Drawing to it,
Growing from it,
Concreting,
Creating,
Community.

Catherine Saunders

CONVERSATION

Hallo I said,
Haven't seen you for a while.
It's me ol' legs
Playin' me up.
He said.
Well how did you get into town,
I said.
I cam' on me boik,
Me ol' car lets me down,
He said
You be careful,
I said
I' be OK
But I do 'ave a bit a trouble
Getting me leg over!

Jennifer Greenway

GLOUCESTERSHIRE GIRL

A country girl is what I am, country born and bred
The child did not appreciate it, thought it rather dead
A city dweller I became in my early teens
Life was harder for me, it wasn't what I'd dreamed

Fate it was, that brought me back, when barely twenty one
Back here to the Cotswolds, where life had first begun
Seeing it through new eyes, now that I'd settled down
The Severn and the rolling hills, the little market towns

Suddenly all beautiful the country sights to me
Elvers from the river, wild flowers and blackberries
Picnics in the summertime, outings to the Malverns
Shopping trips to Gloucester, the bore along the Severn

Berkeley has it's castle with visitors galore
Slimbridge and the Wetlands Trust, geese and ducks and more
We raised our little family the years how they just flew
The Vindi training ship lived and died, the power station too.

We can't get Elvers nowadays, the market towns have changed
The motor car gets everywhere and folk are not the same
Yet all along the country lanes and high up on the hills
Peace and beauty can be found and pride to make the heart swell.

Rona M Coe

RECAPTURED

This morning a knot
of mere men on the pavement
with brown paper parcels
were clutching at life
while the string and the wrapping
by fraying and bulging
was making a showing
of coming apart.

As for the time being
the gates slammed behind them
and for once on the right side
anxious and dumb
they waited and watched
as a purposeful woman
reclaimed from the wrack
of the Prison
just one.

Ray Flynn

A COUNTRY WALK

In serried ranks
They line the undulating path
A guard of honour
Uniformly green.
Ordered protection
Inviting review.
And closer to the earth
Milk white snowdrops
Harbingers of a long awaited spring
Bend shyly from their slender stalks
In reverence.
The filtered sun
Dapples the ground
And spiked holly
Darker green and stronger
Joins grey - green pines
To make a gentle shade
And oft repeated songs
So sharply trilled
Ring clearly through the pure crisp air.
If there is paradise on earth
Then surely it is here
In this other Eden.

Thelma L Robinson

NEW YEAR 1992

The sea has cast you up,
a wretched, wailing sea creature.
Your back, its spines worn to brittle antennae,
bludgeon touch.

Fear has its own uncharted flesh,
transparent, finely veined, surface scarred.
You gather behind that armour,
that shipwrecked bone.

I saw your eyes once,
frosted like a cocktail glass,
staring at your trembling hands
seized by a grief
that took you away -
- a summer spent drowning
lost in lithium.

Dear, flailing sea creature,
whose only excuse is life,
it's time you came to play.
Spin, spin to the wind's wild willing.
After all, sea spray corrodes
and sand hones the skeleton to a spindle,
eventually.
Even the sea has its prophesies
in its semaphore of birds,
the mouthing of caves
its landed runes upon the shore,
the milking of your jelly flesh.
Its scriptures are in its ebbing and its flowing,
eternally.

Read each word grain by grain,
foretell how in the wasting of the waves
and the wilting of the sand
and the wanting of the hull
our landlocked tongues will thirst for the sea bowl's brine
and your shell shall be stone,
finally.

Christine Aziz

WHEN I WAS YOUNG

When I was young
My heart was gay,
I was so in love
And every day
Brought joy.

The wind blew soft
Upon my cheek
The rain caressed
I did not seek
Any shelter.

I was so happy
By your side
I was so content
I could not hide
My joy.

The wind blew soft
Upon my cheek
I was so young
And in love
Oh Lord

Was it only last week.

Helen Frances Mullins Morley

RESPONDENCES

Art belongs equally to both artist and observer . . .
It is like a promise, it holds us in suspense.
                                    (Cathrin Pickler)

In the Gallery
There is so much the painter does not mention
                              (Elizabeth Jennings)

In a Gallery
We gaze long at paintings, it
is our way with them.

Scanning figured surfaces
Deciphering images,
Collating facts.

But blinkers can slip
And a canvas come alive!
A shock of wonder

Intuitively
Extending our perception
Beyond the given.

Yet fleeting - a haiku-flash!
Consciousness shifting,
Its fullness fading.

Music ending,
Memory of some
Unsustainable completeness.

John Robson

106

A MOPED RIDE TO WORK

Fog wet goggles
Jumper damp
I insect buzz the road to work
To see
Acquaintances of a moment's glance
Tread the pavement path,
Each day forgetting
The journey is endless.
Through the town's diesel sour breath
To the mist infested silence
Of the country lane,
Frost aching fingers
Wrapped around the throttle.

Got to beat the clock
Got to beat the clock
To worship people's bottoms
In the land of office block.

Past the battered rabbit
Past the gypsy site
Fleeing home and family
In the morning's feeble light.

Then down the drive
Dead slow,
To the palace of strip lit windows
That claims near half my fate
But I have gained two minutes
By that, is what I'm late.

Matthew N Hustings

PLEASE! NOT YET THE SPRING

Mud that has no form,
Leaf that has no colour,
Husk that has no seed,
Give me these,
But please not yet the spring
With the searing, soaring beauty of it all;
I am weary and must rest
Where the swirling pattern slides
Down the whirlpool in time's cauldron,
In the space between the years.

Janet Maggs

THE FIRE EATER

Standing in the Square,
He lurches forward; drunk,
Yet still he pulls the crowd.

They are peering around
corners, dodging heads
to watch the drunk
man juggle with
flame torches,
consuming them in his
mouth, releasing the
still burning flame back
into the cold night air.

The fire within explodes
his gunpowder words
stream out abuse
to his audience;
Give me money!
says the fire-eater.

Rebecca Miller

MAN'S INVENTIONS?

The bee and the spider,
Pythagorean by nature,
The former tho' mathematically score
Many aeons long before
The latter came into being.
Belatedly man waves his flag
And to his kind announces
His discovery, which he flounces!
Jet propulsion to man long hid,
Is the easiest thing to do
For the Octopus and squid!
The helicopter, the hovering jet,
The submarine makes a third!
Contemptuously equated
By the whale and humming bird!
Now this . . . it makes me sigh . . .
The silly, overweight bumble bee,
That science says can't fly!
Another contradiction of course,
Is the unique sea horse:
Believe it or not, for what it's worth.
He actually gives birth,
He does from his male groin
His offspring are born!
OK, say I'm mad, maybe you do;
I know I've read it, I believe its true.
Criticism may be easily hurled,
But honestly there's little new in the world
If you think that hard to prove,
Just allow your imagination to move.

Eric Bocking

A RIVER FULL WITH TEARS

See me
along down by the river with a friend.
We would play.
Leaves trail on a ripple's edge,
boats away on Autumn's call.
We would sit upon the notion
that the leaves will lead us home.
If we were ever lost then as idlers
we would roam, down by the river
where we would watch the passing day.
Casting off our own leaves,
bare feet in waters tread
the falling leaves of Autumn cover up the dead.
River seems to sleep, would our shouts awaken it?

Playing by its side our names echo 'cross its banks.
Still waters run forever deep,
names carved upon its silt bed.
Plenty of room for another - victim.

Don't play by the river!

Sailing lollipop sticks, skimming stones,
picking out the dead leaves.
Duane, my friend, stands up high on rotting wood
and feels the autumn breeze.
Splash! his body plunged the deep.
I cried out, not knowing what to do.
On river bed does my friend sleep?

Yet in the final minute comes reprieve,
a passing stranger.
In he dives, retrieves my friend,
so, is the river deprived.

Bringing back my friend,
on the river bank we sat,
made our way home, him like a big drowned cat,
lesson learned!

Our mothers took the view the hard way,
Cross! cold fear voiced words from mother -
the river don't go near.

Antony Gilbert

SPOILT LAND

They are dotted all over these hills,
peculiar hummocks, islands of history,
each with three or four haunted trees,
too neat not to have been planted.
When we arrived I liked their mystery;

on idle days paced their length
or imagined Neolithic monsters.
The black paths should have warned me,
and the names still borne by streets
marking the valley below. These chambers

hold death of a more recent sort.
Coal smooth as Whitby jet
gleams through grass; the soil is tainted,
the spoil of lives. Look with care
and you will find buried rail or sett,

terrace and clearing left unfarmed.
The nettles continue their story,
growing rankest on troubled ground.
Each twisted tree guards a shaft;
earth dips ominously.

In this spoilt land ghosts walk
through garbed in black, not white.
They load panniers, haul buckets.
Winter winds carry their voices;
owls cry their names all night.

Pauline Kirk

OUTSIDERS

Standing segregated like a foreign casualty,
I made some attempt to fit in,
But clearly they wanted to keep their friendship from me,
It's not ambiguous to why I could not win.
Only because I dressed differently and had different ideas.
Just because I did not go wild over a new fashion craze,
I had no fellow peers,
How I shiver like a frightened child when I think of my school days.

Teasing, taunting and cruel name calling shadowed my childhood.
It is now I know that I wouldn't change my appearance even
                                                    if I could,

I recall how they would run around me and tug at my plats,
How they would make noises whispering about me, like the
                                                    hissing of cats,

As I look back upon the unhappy child I was, who contained
                                                    great tolerance

I wonder why my colour made such a difference.

I'm small and fat, I always have been,
Does this give people the right to be mean?
Does this give people the right to call me a pig?
Or to constantly remind me that I am big?
Or to place upon my brow the dunce crown?
Or to label me the class clown?
Or to refuse to have me on their team?
Do I not feel, do I not dream?
Do I not breath, do I not eat?
Do I not cry, does my heart not beat?

Bang! My desk cries as a book is slapped upon it.
Did you do my homework? I hope you've got it.
Of course I had, it was my onus,
I had spent three hours on it, but for this there's no bonus.

I regret having such a good brain,
Why couldn't I be popular, simple or plain?
It's not as I thought it was, being a grade A student,
Especially when you have someone threatening you to do their
homework, who is tolerant?

Jasmin N Blackwood (16)

ON BEING RED

Today I feel different than yesterday.
Woke up, looked in the mirror,
And the blonde had gone.
Replaced by a fiery redhead.
A whole new persona.
I shook my head for this was new territory for me.
Put on a burgundy dress to match,
Smiled a little at the small pale face looking back at me
And thought, 'I've found myself again.'
That young girl from another decade was back -
Wearing my shoes but with a few more lines etched.

I do feel more vampish.
And sultry. And a tad more intelligent.
As if to prove this I stopped by the library.
Bought an *Adult Education* book.
Perused it in my lunch hour.
I could throw pots, creatively write, learn self-hypnosis,
practice Tai Chi.
But I'll probably end up doing none of these things
And just go back to examining my left toenail.
And crying a little.
For the wasted years.
And for the peroxide blonde
Who stopped cars,
That is no more.
Just a bespectacled redhead
In the wake of life.

Karen Dick

113

JUST SEVENTEEN

Growing up is never easy,
I will tell you what I mean.
Please try to understand me,
Now I am seventeen.

When I am feeling moody,
You are angry as can be,
But when I help, you seldom say,
How pleased you are with me.

You say that I'm untidy,
So I work all Sunday through.
You never say, *Your room looks nice.*
But, *It's about time too.*

When I put on my make up,
You say I look a mess,
You never like my style of hair,
Or even how I dress.

With stiletto heels and pencil skirt,
Your mum did not agree,
Remember, Mum when you were young,
Before you pick on me!

You ask me where I'm going,
And add, *Don't be home late*
You never say, *Did you have fun!*
Did you enjoy your date?

Dad says I must try harder,
For life is not just fun.
How often does he pat my back,
And say, *Good luck, well done.*

I got many hugs and kisses,
When I was very small.
I still need that affection,
Although I've grown so tall.

114

I know that you both love me,
But you seem afraid to say.
I try to show I love you too,
In my own peculiar way.

Perhaps we'll get on better,
Now my problems you have seen.
I love you and I need you,
Now that I am seventeen.

Dorothie E Stalton

ATTEMPTED RECOLLECTIONS

Who are you, your face I do not recall.
Why do you stare so intently, your eyes.
I am afraid, of what I cannot comprehend.
My mind I attempt to stimulate, think, think.
Those lost years, how long have I lived?
Where has time gone
stolen, disintegrated, yet
faded pictures fleetingly rise to the fore,
dim greys, blurred images mouthing silent words.
I strive to recognise those features as I gaze at your face,
your eyes, who are you, should I recognise or know?

Papers you hand me, documents you say,
jumbled meaningless words,
symbols etched, what do they mean?
These fatigued eyes of mine cannot transcribe.
Reflections you relate of a life fully lived,
I'm sorry I cannot recall.
Please leave me alone to rest in peace,
no more questions probing into my brain.
I'm tired, so weary but tell me please,
I need to know,
who are you, your face, I do not recall

Avril M Common

THE SONG OF THE TRAPPED ONE

wait, wait!
let me unlace my boots
and leave them behind,
boots, heavy -
rooting me to this mountain top
of practical life and its details,
this everyday market place
where people come out to sell themselves

I will not glance behind
with regret
no, not even a dust particle of it,
I will take a long
last gasp, then

I will will myself to jump off
this cliff edge,
leave this gallery
of family and friends

wait, wait!
my river,
my love,
floating, you -
your light being - me
unwinged, you glide winged-like
looking up, I can still see you
I see you
still
among the rapids
nimble
you fly through the rocks
angelfish
in your translucent lilac-blue
white wrapping

I follow you
with all my being
my boots
almost off,
and you
almost out of sight.

Basia Palka

THE IRREVERSIBLE

There's no path back to years gone by,
We see them in our memories eye.
That road we trod when we were young,
The taste of life sweet on our tongue,
Unheeding youth with time to burn,
Cannot go back; cannot return
To change a single hour or day
Which we wasted on the way;
To find the place or face we know
From the past, so long ago.
Time travels on a one way track,
Forward only, no going back.
We can't rewrite the life we've led,
Choices made or things we've said.
We can't erase a single word,
However thoughtless or absurd.
It's written in our past and we
All spend our time so carelessly.
Each minute is a one way door,
We think that there are plenty more.
But time runs out; one day it's spent
And we wonder where the years all went.
Time may be infinite, but, my friend,
Our lives are not; they have an end.

Evelyn Hoath

THE APPIAN WAY

There is a fair and ancient street,
Where e'er I longed to place my feet:
To Rome, that once imperial seat,
Doth lead the Appian Way.

This road is now a place of dread
The screaming planes rise overhead,
And speeding cars would strike me dead,
Within the Appian Way.

But now I hear another sound
The *trudge, trudge, trudge* of cohorts bound
For their great city, far renowned,
Along the Appian Way.

Their brass, their shields and spear tops glint,
Their boots the mud on cobbles print,
And faces Rome-ward set as flint
Upon the Appian Way.

Triumphant generals urge them on
Whilst in the town expectant throngs
Of wives and children raise the song
'Look to the Appian Way!'

Come roll the chariots and siege-mounts tall,
Make haste the slaves, the booty, all;
Rome's mystic charms her children thrall
About the Appian Way.

Yet now I see a fearsome sight,
Look! Human torches rend the night
As martyrs blaze their witness bright
Beside the Appian Way.

At them the marchers mock and rail
But even seasoned warriors fail
To heed that unseen Hosts prevail
Around the Appian Way.

So "Bab'lon's" vaunted arches ring
As praise to Nero maidens sing,
But he's long dead and Christ is King,
Despite the Appian Way.

Michael Lee

INHERITANCE

We discuss the name, divide it in to syllables
And guess its derivations.
Our daughter says it is from Norway

And you produce the evidence
Finding photographs of blond cousins,
Remembering your brother

But you are dark and foreign looking
And our daughter has been taken
For something else, Italian or French

And your mother's father they say
Was Welsh. So we examine ancestry
Our place in it and what we know of it,

And look for talents in our children,
Miracles, and say they are not ours
But are a gift from our

Progenitors when the unexpected thing
Breaks out. But for your mother she was
As much at home in Lancashire

As she might have been in Wales,
Taking your father's name. But it is certain
That you are all musical

And your eyes are the same, brown
As the peat dark water
Running down from the hills.

Josephine Haslam

GRANDMA MAY

There I saw the ghost of Grandma May,
Sitting at the end of my bed one day.
She scared me so, the shock knocked me dead . . .
Now I sit with Grandma May at the end of my bed!

Soman Balan

YAD VASHEM

And G-D looks down

Limpid pools lap on ancient stones
Sun baked sky looks down on flowers
That bloom through cranied walls
Crunch of gravel from walking feet
Drawn on and on towards a sacred shrine

And G-D looks down

Serenity pervades the air
Yet silence speaks
Its own lamenting sound
The azure blue above
Greyed by a passing plane
A bird takes fright
And wings its way
To safety far beyond

And G-D looks down

Enter the hall of horror friend
Prepare your eyes
Your mind, your heart
The purple light
Tells its own reason
For being just one light
That burns for six million souls

And G-D looks down

At last you are there
Looking into eyes that stare
From skeletal frames
Behind barbed wire fencing
The soul screams within
As the transfixed gaze
Absorbs the scene of bones
That once held men
Oh G-d of mercy
Why, why

And G-D looks down

A father takes his son's hand
The child sees
Only *pictures* on the walls
'Glidder Abba' he requests
Oppressed only by the heat of the day
The scene is passed
But the mind is scarred
By what might have been
As the man relives the visions
Of *Gehenim*
Through which he has just passed

And G-D looks down

A dog barks
the flowers are blooming
Children laughing
People talking
The child's *Glidder*
Smears his face as he walks
Beside his tear stained father
Into his unknown future

And G-D looks down.

Genya Kutchin

WAITING UPON THE WEAVING

Must be
　That the Gods are sleeping,
Our dreams
　In their safe keeping,
Precious moments
　Fleeting,
Waiting
　Upon the weaving.

Gerald Aldred Judge

THE CRUCIFIX

I stood alone - and gazed in awe.
Could I behold a fairer sight?
I gazed upon a window rare -
A stained glass window, crowned in light.
I saw the Saviour on the cross.
His face was sad, His brow was torn,
His hands were pierced by cruel nails.
He wore a crown of bramble thorn.
The Holy Virgin from below,
Sat, looking at His tortured face.
Thinking perhaps the Son of God,
Should never have come to this sad place.
The vision faded, 'ere my eyes
Could look too well on sacred scene
Of Calvary where Jesus Christ
Was crucified upon the green.
And there was I - stood in the nave
Of a lovely church, though small,
Gazing at the face of Him,
The Lord who saved us all.

Enid Rathbone

SUICIDE ON SILWOOD

2nd January, the year had just begun,
what did you fear
what happened in the old one
to make you want to disappear.

The ninth floor, the last place you stood
what thoughts crossed your mind
as you looked down to the ground,
did life really treat you that unkind.

Somerfield House, the place from where you jumped,
was you lonely, is that what made you depressed?
Was there no-one to see?
No family that could have guessed.

Is life so fragile
did your mind snap
like a flower in the wind
was you in a never ending trap.

Did you watch others celebrate
Christmas and New Year
was you sad and lonely
while others were full of good cheer.

Are we so blind in this day and age
we can't see when another human needs aid?
Was you one of life's forgotten folk
one of the bottom grade?

Did we walk past you
not giving a second thought?
Or is there nothing no-one could have done?
Is your death no-one's fault?

Are we free from guilt
are our consciences clear
as to what made you take your life?
I guess we'll never hear.
J J Brooks

PTE AKERMAN D. 1917

And should you pass the ancient church
with flint faced walls of a spireless tower,
whereupon the village clock accuses heaven
at the midday hour.
And out through the graveyard where
spirits flew,
an overgrown tangle of cornflower blue.
And onto the lane and down to the square
where the bronze to the fallen
stands proudly there.
And should you enter the dimlit shadows
of the thatched and timbered inn
and order a mug of Suffolk ale
to drown your dreams of glory in,
then settle upon settles of time stained oak,
'neath roughcast walls, yellow with smoke.
And should the church clock start its chime,
then remember me . . .
                    in another time.

Brian Clark

THE BIKER

He came into the bar, clad all in leather, deep and black,
With studs upon his jacket and an eagle on his back,
His hair was long and wavy and his smile, a lazy grin,
His boots were black, with straps on and I fell in love with him.

His glance was cool and casual as he gazed around the bar,
His manner was so laid back as his hand closed around his jar,
I wondered where he'd come from, a stranger in this place,
I moved a little closer so that I could see his face.

He turned and then he saw me, and his eyes looked into mine,
Hello there was his greeting, I think I said I was fine.
We chatted for a while, but all the time my heart beat fast,
I think he felt the same way and how quick the evening passed.

He offered me a ride home, I was quick to answer *Yes,*
The gleaming motorcycle, with the wind beneath my dress,
The road, a silver ribbon, sped beneath the cycles wheels -
And the headlights came towards us as I heard the brakes
                                                    that squealed.

I can't recall the impact or the sound a crash must bring,
I can't recall the pain, nor yet the sound of death's dark wings,
But I can see again the scene, of him and I, below,
Before he took me by the hand, before we turned to go.

Joan Wheeler

JUST FOR THE KIDS

Tinsel invades our ordered world again
Festive season's obligations require
Annual strategies back into play
Input, collaboration, action plans, deception.

Gotta-do-it! Go-to-it! Nothing-to-it!
Go-through it! Gotta-get-through-it!

Paper strewn carpet's bed of roses
Cries of joy from ecstatic poses
Shining white under glowing noses
We did it! we suppose.

Exhausted eyelids inevitably fall
Young bundles cradled upstairs to dream

And we?
Love's mystery solved
Flopping back, glass-in-hand
We punch the remote . . .
Normal service was resumed as soon as possible.

Until next time . . .

Bernard Reay

ALICE AND THE CRESS BEDS

Some girls for reasons of their own won't speak to boys. Alice
                                       was one.

Alice was twelve. She came to the village for holidays like us
(her aunt was widowed and had her down to stay).
I'd met Alice once before but heard she had her own friends;
anyone in their teens was too old to bother with.
She dressed like an ancient Egyptian with frocks to her feet
and adopted a sideways walk to suit the fashion.

It was on the way home from Merden Meadows, I remember.
The road runs there along the Birren tow path.
Alice got up out the of the stream where I found her
With bulrushes in both hands and indescribable cresses in all
                                       her pockets.

It isn't the way I usually find girls:
I'm afraid I may have given the wrong impression. I said
Is there anything I can do to help? Not that I could
because there are several things I'd rather help than wet
                                    Egyptians. Anyway
she went back into the water and made off downstream
heading, I think, for Thebes and the Temple of Karnak.
Then I lost sight of her round Willows Bend.

It's odd how being uncomfortable takes people.
I had to go straight home and change into a dry suit.

Roland Portchmouth

GARDEN OF SECRETS

Why do you fail to look beyond the obvious?
Is it so hard to trim the velvet?
I know you say troubles have echoes,
But in this hallowed place of empty wedding vows,
You can't wear your heart on your sleeve.

I touched you and I felt afraid.
In the garden of secrets,
I lifted the floorboards and discovered the void.
Then I pitied the land that needed a hero,
As this was a capital without a country.

A jewelled citadel, trapped forever in the lava light.
An aborted Utopia, a stain amongst the heavens.
Nothing grows here anymore,
Life only festers and decays.
Yet that night I wanted to stay forever.

'Well my precious, we tried our best dear,
I could have said more given more time.
But the hour has come for me to leave,
And I depart at first light.'
It is an experience I will remember . . . but not now.

Matthew Kirk

BEFORE THE WEDDING DAY

I think it was September when they said they'd named the day -
And oh! My goodness, since that time it's been *anchor's* away
What once was called a sitting-room is now an antique shop
It's filled with boxes, pots and pans, from bottom to the top.

We've had so many secrets, it's been, 'Don't tell this or that,'
But I felt that it had gone too far when we had to gag the cat!
We've shopped for bits of ribbon, from here to Timbuktu -
Oh! Then there was the garter - now should it be pale blue?

There's a big box filled with groceries, and every little thing,
I know they'll have some gravy, and they'll eat just like a king
But now at last the day is here, the honeymoon all planned
And though we're feeling shattered - we'll not join them on the sand

We'll wait until the van pulls up, the rest of things to take,
So now - here's to the newlyweds, God bless, please cut the cake.

Trudie Crossan

EXILE - HOMAGE TOM PAULIN

I scratch my arse as I lie
In the bath and beyond
The window the whole
Of England lies bored.

Soon I will recall the scrawl
Of the past - perhaps September
That sentient month translated
Into flight.

Root-fret-soft-bank and foliage
Green. Sun honey-clear.
Was it not quite paradise
As rainbow skies fell-

Was it not the one crystal time
Of unclenched rhyme.

Time hardens the present
And the window upon which
I gaze is a blackened
Suture.

An isolation burns my ear.

O requiems stiffen
Your holy name
My love

My what was once country -
Cauled and petrified
I have seen you go-
I have spun a golden web
Against your woe.

I scratch my arse as I like...

John Donaghey

THE FLOWER BOUTIQUE

Open the door to Flowerland.
Angel chimes proclaim: the firm you trust!
Miss Daphne Bloom, the floral landscapist!
Roses, freesias, lilies, myosotis,
Lovingly displayed in pewter jugs,
Instant delivery at your behest.

Open the door to Flowerland.
Flower power has more strength than words.
Daphne's violet eyes scorn credit cards.
Try the sundries, add those extra touches,
Flowers with chocolates or teddy bears . . .
Close the door gently, let the angels rest.

Patricia Lucas

THE FIRST EASTER

There are daffodils dancing in gardens,
In woodlands, in dales and on knowles.
        Were there daffodils there, at Calvary
        When a man paid a price for our souls?

There are blackbirds and thrushes and sparrows
Nest building and singing with glee
        Were there birds singing that day at Calvary
        When they nailed very God to a tree?
There's a promise of summer and sunshine,
Of warm, balmy air, blessing soft.
        Was the air sweet and kind there at Calvary
        When they lifted the Christ from the cross?

Easter Sunday dawned and they pondered,
Where was He and who moved the stone?
        But He rose on the day He predicted
        This Saviour, and came into His own.
Mena Faulkner

OBITUARY

'He was seventeen here.'
The finger lay on a photo -
fading, in an old album.
A boy looked out at me,
round cheeked, a skinny neck
above a khaki uniform -
too large for him.

'This is 1919.'
Her hand stained with age -
lying, on an open page.
A man stared at me,
hollow cheeked, moustached,
three stripes on a khaki sleeve -
ribbons and medals.

'He would never say.'
She has closed up the book -
secrets clasped within.
Now an old man has died.
Fifty years a milkman,
then, an allotment -
champion at rhubarb.

'But, I knew a hero!'
'Put this in your newspaper.
He was with Haig - Field Marshal Haig.'
'He fought at Passchendale.
Thousands died in the mud.
But, Thomas Atkins survived -
to die in his bed!'

Pat Hennessy

STILL IN THE IRON BAR'S ENCLAVE

Still in the iron bars' enclave
the huddled glitter of disordered day
stipples down as shredded glints
each eon born's thus simpled
to an infant hour
and fritters into dark
by dark's devoured

and all that I was readied to become
by promise fuelled with life
out in the air
and out and out and out of everywhere
no sun should see
nor ever should have seen's
with cold stones pressed to shadows left
to be
forever now
the aftermath
of me

so that I tend to harsher lights
to blend
extinguished love with metal
wrought from ire
to burn unstopped
as any forging fire
through what hearts turned
and gutted my esteem
and spurned as ash
the tinder
of my dreams.

Viv Foster

ONE CALENDAR

They danced in shades of pyramids
and on the stage of the Parthenon.
They danced to the roar of lions in Rome
and to Nietzsche's dream of an Aryan home.
They danced till the flesh fell away from their bones,
as November trees shed leaves.
Now there's no more time for ballet -
the dancer's so believe -
But there's always a piccolo player
who wants to take a chance
that the dancer's have not forgotten - how to dance.

Beryl Kline

SECRET AFFAIR

Rosie took the wrong road, now she's lost her soul
Tried to live the wild life, too soon she lost control
She thought she had the answer, shooting for the stars
Look into the mirror girl, can you see the scars
'Cos now there's only shadows, where the sun used to shine
Rosie, do you know I'm here? Or am I wasting my time

'Come into my parlour,' said the spider to the fly
Hey Rosie did you struggle, did you even try?
Like a phantom of the opera, you hide behind a mask
And you're breaking all the mirrors, that remind you of your past
'Cos now there's only shadows, where the sun used to shine
Rosie, do you know I'm here? Or am I wasting my time

You tried to keep things secret, but Rosie I'm aware
The dangerous game you're playing, you say it's your affair
You're giving me the answers, the questions never asked
But all I have to go on, is the history of your past
And now there's only shadows, where the sun used to shine
Rosie do you know I'm here? Or am I wasting my time

Victor Bing Havard

HOME BASE

As daylight draws to a close,
As the voice of God over mighty waters
Begins to whisper,
To usher in the Sabbath Queen,
Army routine comes to a standstill.

A four-directional peace:
To the north, tired soldiers' canons,
Against the backdrop of the snowy Hermon Mount
With her night illuminations
Blasted by the pillar of fire
That leads the camp.

Veering eastwards, greenery and puddles;
Up into the mountains and then into
Creamy, cloudy ellipses of cotton wool,
Suspended in mid-air with relaxed tranquillity.

Towards Jerusalem, cows grazing - their calm reticence
Reflecting the inner peace of a city full of people and problems
On the Sabbath Day Herself.

Westwards, the golden sunlight hiding behind the crevices,
Basking in her energised, beneficent glow.

And as the Sabbath creeps in,
The sun begins to fade, the cows continue to munch,
The puddles ripple silently, the tensions of soldiers slowly unwind;

As nature, Soldier, City,
Prepare to receive the face of the Sabbath.
Each according to its, his, her needs,
Yet united by the Day's harmony,
Bringing peace between contradictory worlds,
Nature and Man, on Home Base.

Jonathan A Jackson

COSMIC HEART

The Holocaust's pall
depicted
On an exhibition wall

Bared bones evoking
groans
Horror and despair
Ours
to bear

Time cannot efface
Humanity debased
Wrought in gold
heritage unfold
Kiddish cup and praying shawl
Where are they all?

Bud and blossom trees in
Spring
Children's murder sing
Innocent eyes rise above the
funeral pyres
Memorial light
ignite
Their darkest night

From the grave
Massada
Not the slave
Judea
does not depart
Within the cosmic heart

Rita Brisk

CONDOM CONUNDRUM

Shoulder to shoulder back to back
brothers and sisters in a plastic sack
butcher baker candlestick maker
prophet priest catholic quaker
mechanic milkman master of scrolls
defender of honour scorer of goals
robber racist redundant miner
vagrant tinker captain of a liner
red coated huntsman out to kill foxes
smelly inhabitant of old cardboard boxes
winchman hangman judge on the bench
gay intellectual translator of french
victim vandal farmer fag
honourable seventeenth earl in drag
bastard bitch warlock witch
dictator typist drunk slob
father of evil child of god
acrobat on the end of a rope
the man who killed the pope.
But luckily not me.

Kevin Brewer

JONES THE COAL

Jones the Coal holds court,
Streaks the blue skies Tryfan way,
He shows no malice, save a wicked cackle,
As he tumbles, topsy-turvy,
Mocking in his bee-line defiance of five ropes gravity.

Jones the Coal, rampant in posture,
To survey the boundaries the playful black angel,
Simply flipping, rushes the valley floor,
His wings a tool, alter the perspective,
Of fools atop his bastion who bring him charity.

Richard Hudson

135

SO THEY WON'T HAVE TO FIGHT AS MUCH

I am woman, female, girl.
A lady of determination
Independent,
not to be side glanced or ignored.
I am a woman, here today
alive and kicking.
Why kicking?
To be heard, I have to shout,
to see I have to push and shove
'cause I am female,
lesser,
and so I kick and fight,
for myself, and others like me,
for future generations,
of women, females, girls.

Sarah Masters

THE WHITE DESERT

I had heard of the white desert
But did not believe it existed,
Except in the imagination.
Like a huge ghost, it continued to
Haunt me, until one day it was there,
A vast distance of brilliant whiteness.
A slight vibration gently disturbing the atmosphere.
This was the land of the unseen,
A place of invisible promise,
Full of plans innumerable
And of intense activity.
Here, in the vast whiteness
Are created wonders to come.

Norman Oakes

RECOLLECTION

I remember
names and places: habits
that throw people
into relief.
I remember
events and conversation:
words that excite,
emotions that pulsate.
I remember
plotting my past and
future: seeing myself
in simple situations,
discussing deals and prices.
I remember
everything I've forgotten:
I store experience
in case of emergency.

Matthew Russell

THE BELL

In the silence of St Stephen
's night
Christmas lay dead,
Waked in a street of litter
Indulgence satisfied;
Sleepless in a morgue of coloured lights
I heard an ancient bell,
In barren silence broken
The matins hour tolled,
Calling the Cistercians
Through centuries to prayer;
Then I prayed, with ageless men,
In Portglenone before the dawn.

W McCann

DEAR MR TELETHON

Dear Mr Telethon,
Just thought I'd let you know
That what you say about us
Really isn't so.
We may not all be perfect,
We might not use our legs,
But that doesn't make us rejects
Nor should we have to beg
For scraps from off your table,
For slices of your cake,
Whilst all the while being labelled
(Between commercial breaks)
As needful of your charity,
Your pity and your shame,
When all we want is parity:
To be treated just the same.
So come on Mr Telethon,
I hope you get my drift.
It's time to end this marathon,
And give us rights not gifts!

Darren P Chanter

HAIKU

The circle completes
  and I am next to you now
in the mystery.

Others do not hear
  the joy that sings inside us
as we join our hands.

You are a circle:
  with your arms you embrace me
in the spiral dance.

Judith Israel

JERUSALEM

Standing in Jerusalem
I hear poetry,
Great symphonies playing.
I stand in Jerusalem
Listening.
The old and new blend,
Burn in the Dome of the Rock
With the fire of the overhead sun.

I walk to the soldiers' resting place,
In the same steps as the bereaved.
The trees reach upwards.
There is stillness
But where I walk the ground is stained.
Abraham, Isaac and Jacob are with me.
I pray by the Wall.
Chanted psalms linger in the air.
I am standing in Jerusalem.

Valerie D Cohen

MISSING PERSON

A haunting voice, a soulless sound,
Blows around my lonely bed
The tender wind is whispering
The words you always left unsaid

Elusive as your absent form,
The moonlight shivers, icy white,
Its slender fingers stroke my skin
With a touch of winter light

I sleep within the arms of night
And dream that they belong to you
Holding me and showing me
The kind of love I never knew

Jennifer Williams

139

UNTITLED

Our dear ideals are cheaply bought and sold
In marketplaces made of broken dreams;
Cliché abounds,
And to our cost, we find the words come dear.

The cowering form of truth is hidden
In a corner, underneath the eaves:
Blinded and gagged,
The dust of ages piles upon its brow.

An exodus in the wilderness is all our life:
A crying in the desert, on the dusty air,
Is all we hear.
Our ears are closed to the quiet core of being.

Muriel Inganni

MAKING THE BEETROOT SOUP

A simple recipe for soup,
In Yiddish in a fading script,
'Take beetroot, lemon juice and egg . . .'
Familiar formula for borscht.

I grasp the nubbed root in my hand,
Sharp strokes bite keen through yielding flesh,
Bright juices spurt across the board
And entrails spatter on the floor.

Rank blood and marrow fill my pan,
Death's sweet-sour stench seeps through the house,
A Dybbuk belches forth from steam
And writhes in frenzy round the room.

A simple recipe for soup,
Dark guilt assuaged with acid tears,
White shells disgorge new life, new hope -
Warm liquid curdles and congeals.

Maureen Sandler

OCTOBER MORNING

Smokers take their last drag.
Those already seated, stamp their feet,
Thankful they thought
To bring their gloves.
Someone calls across the aisle
'Should have brought
A blanket Lil'
A word and smile
From the coach driver
Shirt sleeved.
'Must be hot blooded'
Then silence
As we glide past unbelievable
Beauty, hills, lakes,
God painted leaves
On trees that cast
Frost icing shadows
On the grass.
And we
Strangers whose lives have touched
Become one in infinity.

Dorothy Genower

LEAVING

She leaves her desires and dreams behind,
In the empty house,
With echoing rooms,
That never really knew laughter.
A lingering look,
Before she turns the key,
For the last time,
and picks up the suitcase,
and the remnants of her life.

Julia A Smith

141

IF ONLY!

Together we sat in the side room
Grandmother, Mother and I,
United in our grief for the baby who had died.

'She was so brave, sister, seldom cried
Always seeming to smile
A gentle sweet smile of wonder. Isn't that right Gran?'

Memories were kindled, lit with love
As the milestones they recalled
Of her short cherished oft painful nine month life.

'Remember Gran her small puckered face
Licking her first ice-cream?
Then with bright eyes and clapping hands she begged for more.'

'And chocolate' said Gran, 'Remember the mess,
Tasting it with pleasure
Spreading it over hands face and clothes with laughter?'

'Doctor told us after her birth
Our only child she would be
We were content because we knew all our care she needed.'

I waited with them and understood
Yet thought of another little one
With tremulous smile and haunting eyes which appeared to plead,

'Don't hit me please like my mother did
For sobbing and crying one night
One night at home when she wanted to watch the Telly!'

My heart sobbed with silent sobs
Yearning - if only I could play just once
Santa Claus or *God*.

Betty Morgan

142

BOSNIA 1993

Stuttering rifles, rubble of houses, boys
Cowering to kill, be killed by yesterday's friends,
Obeying what call? Dying to serve what ends?
What uncle gave these fine death-slavering toys?
They say you must buy freedom with your blood,
Alien intruders must be overthrown.
But when it's done, who then will come to own
Your lives, your loves, your homes, this sea of mud?

Not you, dear boys, but those who hold you cheap,
Igniting in your ardent breasts the hate
To murder old and young. They will create
A pen for men they've shrunk to mindless sheep.
Power and gain - are these forever more
To drag sick world through corpse-filled swamps of war?

Terence Moore

IDLERS

Under darkening walls,
When the first cars jockey in the county car-parks,
Beating the early rush,
And mainly sticking to sidelights -
When the suits come out,
And attendant faces calculate
Time and distance home,
And leaves begin to settle in edges and corners,
And the shop windows start to come into their own,
And - look! - a television crew with a fluffy zeppelin,
And all or nothing happened all day all over town -
Then we say:
'Let's check Situations Vacant just once more tonight to see
If 100-eyed Argus has a bone for me.'

Catherine Hildyard

143

BUTTERFLY MIND

Budleia is intoxicating.
I heard the Admiral say,
'I am reluctant to weigh anchor.'
The Comma replied,
After a slight hesitation,
'If I were a full stop
I should stay here for ever.'
'No place for me,'
Flirted the Painted Lady,
Eyeing the Common Sailor.
Brassy Ringlets and Hairstreaks
Know all the sorrow of parting.
A small voice admitted
To feeling a Little Blue.
'Pray don't describe us by colour,
Almond-eyed, dusky or brown -
Too much about race,'
Said the Tortoise, 'Hell!'
A trifle unhinged,
The Gatekeeper had locked himself in.

Gabrielle Billings

A SOLITARY FIGURE

A solitary man, standing with his friends.
Searching for beginnings, and finding only ends,
Following lines forward, forgetting that time bends.
A solitary figure, standing with his friends.

A solitary man, staring at the sky.
Wishing for a future, watching clouds go by.
He doesn't want to do it, but he has to try.
A solitary figure, staring at the sky.

A solitary man, crying for the dead.
Memories of summer days are fighting in his head,
For a long forgotten and where angels fear to tread.
A solitary figure crying for his dead.

A solitary man, talking with his love.
Never makes the right move, no matter what he does.
He wants some intervention from the spirit up above.
A solitary figure, talking with his love.

A solitary man, living in the past.
Refusing to acknowledge that perfection couldn't last.
Wanting just to cling to every stone that's cast.
A solitary figure, living with his past.

Dan Wilson

ANOTHER DAY

Behind a screaming
Crowd
Graffiti echoes

Another promise
Fulfilled
By the party's colours

One more glory boy
Laid
In bits, for nothing

Then the pigs
Arrive
Disgorging squaddies

Who pick up the
Pieces
In plastic bags

And that's how it always is.

J M Parker

SILHOUETTE

Silhouette of a man,
was it his plan,
to enter this place,
to steal and take,
all that he can.

Silhouette of a fish,
which darts about,
the hunger that it must banish.
Thrown from side to side,
with a flick of its tail,
head held high it catches its prey,
a fly.

Silhouette of a bomb,
Bang another town gone.

Silhouette of a preacher,
but he's no teacher.
With a soul searching speech,
he pulls at your money,
like a bloodsucking leach.

P F Masterson

BURIED 1889

Thunder rumbling, loud cracks as lightening
reflects on wet tombstones.
St Beuno's secret - 'neath this unmarked grave,
tales repeat a 'killers bones.'
This sodden ground, lit yet seconds
by a flashing streak.
St Beuno's secret may reveal
the 'Whitechapel's Murderer' lies beneath.

Margaret Turner

TURNED TO THE PLOUGH

I feel his heat, standing here next to him.
The chains clink against each other,
And the leather harness is white with salt.
His veins stand boldly, pumping warm blood,
Warm in contrast to the chill air,
That shows his snorting breath,
As jets of pressured steam.
Sweat rolls freely down his brave chest,
While in contrast his gentle eyes survey me,
As heavy as a car he is,
But as gentle as a butterfly.
He stands patiently, waiting for a signal,
Powerful, noble, gentle, loyal,
Forever unquestioning.
'Walk on' I call, and stand aside,
To watch in wonder, such grace and power,
Turned to the plough.

Neil Roberts

PICTURESQUE

As I look into the myriad mirrors the segmented petals fall,
Like a melba toast that is dripping butter, drip, drip, drip,
A blackbird bobbing about on the sill outside, chirps softly,
A kitten on the window watching the blackbird, purrs loudly.
The light is coming from the moon, reflecting attractively,
Enhancing all my view, making me see everything so clearly.
The day goes on, the sun is shining through the open window,
Creating a warm glow through the open window in my small home.
As I stand still, calmly transfixed by the outside world,
I am startled by the drop of a letter off the postman.
The sweet, yet powerful smell of roses attracts a bumble bee,
As it ignores the delicate, mild fragrance of my bluebells.
The sky is clear, not a cloud in sight, not a drop of rain.

Barbara Lynch

147

SOUL-FRIEND

A secret self, within a self,
A self unseen by others,
save partly glimpsed in searching look
and tender gaze of lovers,
when eye meets eye and keenly scans
the windows of the soul to see,
who'll meet with whom, and when, and where,
a place which needs no key.
Love slips inside, no need to hide
the clutter there which others see.
From room to room they run, carefree,
and share a vocal surrogacy,
whereby a thought, conceived by one,
is given birth through other's tongue.
No vandal here, but loving touch,
caressing treasures loved so much
And even pain of memory
is healed in mirror'd eternity.
In attic of mind and cellar of soul
they glimpse those things which make man whole,
but on the point of taking grasp,
to possess this knowledge of what is true,
they find a *further* place to pass
with only room for one, not two.
In grief they part, no more to share
such fellowship - too much to bear
is joy and sorrow's double face
as each regards that dreadful place.

Betty Hill

WHAT WE LIKE?

Chocolate chilled
Frozen maybe
Delicious biting
Crisp and brittle.
Cool tall beer
Cold and reflective
Rolls down the throat
Soothing and wet.
Art devine
Malicious or sublime
Hard reactions
No-one escapes.
Smooth lover
Wanton forever
Beautifully surrendered
Pleasure and pain.
Elements serene
Wild or ravenous
Mother Earth
Her centuries turn.
War!
Biting cold
Malicious pain
For centuries no contrast
No this and that
No description
Just a bloody inscription
War!

Andrew P Childs

STORMSEEKER

All day we have waited
Sweaty and slow, for some relief
The promised rain, the promised storm
To break through this oppressive haze,
Push back this heady high
To Germany, or Scandinavia.
All day in limbo, waiting
Yet no radical shift on the chart appears
Over England nothing moves, stirs
Or changes, life goes on
And night comes.
Still here I am, watching
Waiting for that first flash
The first sign of the thunder
Brash and loud, head-banging
Against the horizon.
Dim witted and heavy handed
Thigh slapping, beard shaking
Doing the business, ripening crops
Everyone's friend
Going through the motions, of caring
For each and every little man.
A god, yet not quite a respectable
Kindred spirit, familiar old Thor
A bit of a bumpkin, all brawn
Wayward hammer and rough peasant boots
Always trying to achieve the impossible
Balance, but never quite making it
Forever the outsider,
Doing the best he can.

Margaret Cook

UNTITLED

There's a light
That surrounds us
But we can't see it
Our bodies
They're black
Features
Non-existent
Just like our ancestors
So dark
Shadows of the past
Slowly fading
Degrading
Being devoured by the light
The light that will shine
Forever
Into the depths
Of our morbid souls.

Joe-An M

INVOCATION

Hist, vast and hoist!
Crumble your craws!
Leg down the vaunts
Full draw the cree!

Ne'er fall the spit,
Nor shine the blee,
Till manion's glow,
Fills land and sea.

To warble now
Or, flet your splain!

J Winn

WAR: THE ABSTRACT - PILOTS OF SPRING '91

Running wild,
Fur around the fish tank
Feathers on the floor,
Claw marks on the ceiling
Teeth marks on the door,
Eyes are to the keyhole
Ears to the wall,
The Coliseum's on the TV
Open to all.

Fish and Ram roam the sky,
The burden's over pigs don't fry,
Elephants, Lions, Donkeys leave
The Cat and Mice to fight
for the cheese.
Eyes are to the keyhole
Ears to the wall,
Observing the rampaging,
Pass the soap and water,
Round the world.

Paul Hichens

AND THE ROOM SHRANK

A closed door.
A darkened room.
'Close the door as you leave,' she said
'And turn out the lights'
As a yellow butterfly kissed the end of her cigarette.
'Go down the stairs and out the front and keep going'
As a wedding veil hid her half-open mouth
'Don't stop and don't look around'
As the smoke made her eyes sting
And the room shrank.

Joseph Briffa

152

SOLITUDE

The world awakes,
emerging through
the silver morning
like the ghost of
a thousand days;

what men have come
and gone in your
silent slumber?
what lovers through
your dreaming stole,
with hearts melting
in the warm uncertainty
of a night embrace?
what memories are held
forever in your tumbling
veil?

hang still this
moment in life,
suspend safe forever
the sweet isolation
of my intrusion;

accept and surround me
in this my moment
of solitude,
surround me in this
my silver morning,
surround me
and morning come again.

Roger McDonald

ROOFTOPS

A hundred metres across the football field
Where the boarded up houses stand draped in dirt
An alarm bell rings tirelessly,
Running shrill through this dull day
Like a crack through a crystal glass.
The hard note cuts through the air,
Slices through the stereo and stops the TV dead
And the little back yard boys
Stumbling after breakfast cereal toys
Hang their heads like their battered dogs.
Grey clouds are the guardian angels
That draw close to our rooftops
And breathe rain through our days.
A clothes-line is crammed with oversize skirts
That swing in the rain, untouched
And hang heavy and dejected.
From a car pulling in in the next street down
The radio blares and screams;
Cars and flaking vans sit hunched in driveways,
Backs jutting out like swollen, inconvenient warts.
Two women pull in their children's clothes
And chatter across their concrete gardens,
TV talk in caterwaul voices,
Hair bleached though there is no-one to care.
The ways of this street are carved
Deep under their eyes, but no-one reads.
They never look up at the constant drone
Of the growling motorway three blocks down
That leads the grey way to another grey town.

Jaime Gill

THE ART CRAZE

What a wreck Toulouse Latrec
'Toxicated hits the deck
As Bosh in Hell and then Van Gough
Thwarted cut an earlobe off
Like Klee like Munch (a hunch) was potty
Seurat proved that he was dotty
And take Blake that soul in pain
Cezanne, Manet both insane.

Does 'Lisa smile on what's graffiti
Gauguins girls about Tahiti?
Why does Frans Hals' Cavalier
Whistler when James' Mother's near?
In Spain El Greco went to war
A role-model for Salvador
With dripping clocks in Surrealism
While Pollock Picked Expressionism.

'Angelo had crick-neck-feelings
The sort you get when painting ceilings
Titian too felt under-par
(At ninety-nine I bet you are).

As Grunewald and Correggio
Gave way to Michelangelo
Calder Wood and Giacometti
Warhol's Tin of Heinz Spaghetti.

Yeah Mondrian-man what's a square?
While Schwitters-flitters everywhere
A match for Lowry though Rousseau
With Naive artists and Pablo
And Kline-by-line like Hockney say
Exactly where we are today.

Bill Palmer

AUTUMN

Into the biting cold.
Past the empty car park
Past the tree which is working at making
molehills in the pavement with its roots,
The sky is a silent glow of orange
with a single stretch marked cloud.
The houses so black as to be non-existent
mingle with the sky.
Up to the main road and the silvery warmth
of the car headlights
And the comfort of lives being lived
as they should be.
Here is the glow of the ever present streetlights
Making the dark darker
And the visible strange
Trapping objects like flies in amber
Back along the grubby path
Transversed at intervals
By an equally silent being
Or an intimate group, making their way to their car.
Back to the security of enclosed space
Ergonomically designed as it all is.

Clare Hall

NEW DAY

Reluctantly in fragile light,
The day unfolds in pearl-tinged white,
A whisper away from a velvet night,
All stark and strangely new.

A breath in time and the day moves on,
To meet the purity of dawn,
With spider curtains on the lawn,
All laced with spangled dew.

A rasp of rooks against the sky,
And cockerel screams his haunting cry,
A salute to the dawn and the night must die,
In an amethyst hue.

Nancie Foster

GREEK SUMMER 'FROM HERE TO ETERNITY'

You kissed away the cobwebs from my eyes,
Soothed away frustrations from my brow,
And with your tenderness you blew away my pain,
On a sun drenched shore long ago, forgotten were
those days of winter rain.

Like a traveller in time:
I was Helen, Venus, Aphrodite.
A seductive man was massaging me,
Soothing me with his oils,
Warming my emotional cold,
Calming away my melancholy.

Breathing in the scent of summer,
Feeling excited and enhanced,
You made me feel heady and euphoric,
like a ray of sunshine -
brightening up my life,
rekindling my inner self,
Shielding me from storms to come.

Now all that seems so long ago,
Fluorescent lights blot out the sunset in my brain,
I sense thunder over the horizon,
And the smells of processed life linger,
Far away from the smell of aloe and jasmine
Odysseus is just a dream.

Cath Cunningham

EXPOSURE

Across the faultless ice-eyed dome
a shooting star moves like pain
and lodges into darkness.
Frost falls hoary
stubbling the sleeper's chin,
glassy splinters tattooing
deep as indrawn breath
while phantom-limbed
he drifts way beyond dreaming.

Turned-up greatcoat collars shield
and ears burning for
the pull of air inhaled
are wrapped up deaf.
From a crystal-tight crescent
painted empty,
too carefully defined,
light sinks a sidelong glance,
like a hand proffered
and withdrawn in one -
a gesture coughed from pride.

Katharine Millar

THE MUSE

I can see her, sometimes,
ungraspable, dancing ahead,
a shadow that has come unstitched.

She is Puck, Tinkerbell.
I can hear her laughter ringing
but she never will stop to speak.

I can see her, sometimes.
She does not answer my summons
but, capricious, comes when she will,

158

won't stay out her welcome.
She is nights with sleepless children,
late appointments and time for school.

But sometimes she smiles
benignly on me and, grateful,
I receive the gift she bestows.

I see her clearly then.
She's the lucky silver sixpence,
even, the icing on the cake.

Patricia Jones

RULES FOR WALKING IN PARKS (MEN)

Be careful with your eyes.
Look at the lake, the skies.
Keep away from swings and slides.
Be aware you pose
A threat.
If you find
Yourself behind
A woman
Slow down. Take a seat.
If by chance you meet
Head-on
Avoid infringing her space.
Keep your face
Averted.
As you pass ensure you leave
A metre or more between your sleeve
And hers. Do not smile.
Do not
Say 'Good morning'.

Keep walking.

Ray Pluck

THE WOMAN

I sat on the bus
looking out the window,
sort of lost in the smoke
from my cigarette,
a woman, about twenty,
boarded, sat in front of me,
her eyes were red,
and she had a slight discoloration
on the left side of her face.
I looked out the window,
wished the bus homeward.
A little later, we reached some roadworks,
with a makeshift traffic light on red,
the bus gave a continuous shudder,
as it waited to move on,
making everyone's shoulders
move up and down.
The woman in front of me
looked just like she was laughing,
I knew she wasn't,
couldn't be,
I knew why her eyes were red,
I knew what was wrong with her face,
it was obvious.
I lit another cigarette,
and watched the smoke rings I made,
as the bus moved forward.

Michael Clifton

THE OLD AND THE NEW

My grandad often said to me
'I'll tell you how life used to be,'
I listened with intent and pride
As through the years we took a ride.
Christmas brought him tears of joy
How he treasured every toy,
Once, he got a chocolate train
And a wooden soldier game.

Now and then, the brass band played,
In the park or on parade
Once a year, the fair would come . . .
Bringing side shows, rides and fun.

Then he went to Morecambe Bay,
On a trip, just for the day
He didn't go by train or tram
But travelled in a charabanc.

In his daily working role,
He toiled hard in search for coal
Down the pit he went, quite willing
For to earn his weekly shilling.

I sometimes wonder what he'd say,
If he could see the world today
I think that he would be dismayed . . .
With all the progress we have made.

Catherine A Howard

SATURDAY'S MOTHER

Saturday; best, worst day of the week for her.
Six days have passed, yet nothing much has changed.
A phone call twice a week to keep in touch
Discuss his homework, schoolwork, progress, play.
Repeating still in childlike voice, 'Hi, mum'
Relaying information selected for her ears.
A distant voice yet still so much a part of her.
As albums of her memory flick page by page.
His thirteen years catalogued in her memory
Flashbacks to a time when he was with her.
Sharing conversations, thoughts, ideas.
Reminding of his full-stops in his English.
Enjoying his intellect, mental agility; *himself!*
Still she feels the nagging need to care for him
Un-tempered by the passing of a year.
smile, look your best, mum's always spick and span.
With thumping heart she starts the car -
Anxious for his presence.

Maureen Kirby

EUPHORIA

The rounded breast and well formed thigh, the downy touch
I thought I'd die
with the sheer pleasure of it all, I knew my barriers had to fall
Under the spell of this delight, I couldn't wait until the night
When she was naked I would see, the pleasure she could
bring to me,
With tongue and lips her tastes devour at that one bewitching hour.

To feel the soft touch of her skin, whilst rubbing oil outside, within,
easing tender legs apart, of what joy transcends my heart,
She a fledgling, me so old, but in my hands I will enfold
this wondrous being for my pleasure, herein I'll surely find a treasure,
Experience taste as yet untold especially when the *chicken's cold.*

S M Dunn

162

IMAGES OF REBELLION

A hope lost into darkness,
A tortured, screaming crowd.
A sorrow in their anger,
A silence through the sound.

There's a violence in everyone
A cruel streak to life.
The loss of friends and happiness
Is the demon surgeon's knife.

A wishful dream of freedom,
A dreaming wish for truth.
But a bleak reality of useless toil
Means a cry for bonds to loose.

A hope lost into darkness,
A tortured, screaming crowd,
A sorrow in their anger,
A silence through the sound.

Joy Preece

LIMEHOUSE BLUE

Today at Camden Lock the canal
was a whirl of grey-green malaise.
A bare willow appeared larger, viewed
from the watery, still of the lock basin.

At that moment I recalled how I had
cast away a memorabilia of faint
Imaginings, at Limehouse, one
icy February:

And now I watched silently as
they bubbled in ripples and pools,
from under the partially closed
Lock gate.

Peter Johnston

TO DANIEL

You must have been waiting
The time was just right
You've filled a special place
When my heart was so heavy
When my heart was so sad
Along came this tiny person
To make his voice heard
And his presence felt.

Big round eyes
Perfect fingers and toes
Your skin so soft
With your tiny button nose.

You're becoming very special
Part of my daughter and son
To hold you so tight
Seems so normal to me
I wonder how you'll grow?
I wonder what you'll be?

I will love you forever
And maybe beyond
You've given me strength
And helped me go on
You're the most precious gift
My grandson!

Jan Al-Kudsi

164

ODE TO A SCHOOL FRIEND

May

May, you were my dearest friend;
We ran about together,
And trod that twisted road to school,
No matter what the weather.

That little school lay nestled,
In a valley 'neath a hill;
When I take a trip down *memory lane*,
I think I see it still.

The stone built wall, around the ground,
Where we children used to play;
We chased each other round the top,
I still remember to this day.

Now a little homestead nestles there,
The school, a long gone dream.
Those were by far the happier days
Than richer ones I've seen.

When fate put forth her ruthless hand,
And tore us both asunder,
The miles and years, unheading past,
But our friendship still grew fonder.

I cannot tell you how I felt,
When called to your bedside,
And deep down within my heart
I knew, *fate* would again divide.

But only for awhile dear friend,
As the years are flying faster;
We'll meet again in God's good time,
And reign with Him there-after.

Florence Kerr Parkinson

SIBYL AND THE DOG

"I think I'm in love with him,"
I told her.

She smiled in disbelief
until her candour lasered
and stunned me in my place.

"He's a territorial man," she said
"a warrior on the move,
intent concealed in charm,
love measured by what it rules.
He's a fox who knows the crow
when he's after cheese,
he's a tortoise who knows the hare
when the test is speed,
he's a man who sees a woman
as extension of his throne,
he'll stop to smell her roses
if her garden becomes his own.
he's poisoned by ambition
driven by his greed

If I were you, believe me
I wouldn't take to him."

That night I had a dream of him,
I saw him coming close;
he was princely, sure, and charming
but
his asses' ears were gross!

I rushed outside to foist my sign:
"Beware of Dog," it said
And who should then leap from the bushes but
the grand old dog himself:
Cerberus nodding proudly
his heads of prophecy, fear, and strength.
His growling made me tremble and shook me
to the depths.
I woke up from my vision and
tried to move about
but the weight of midnight's wisdom
draped my heart in doubt.

Nora Mahon Olivares

ON READING SOME LINES BY DYLAN THOMAS

It is so good that poets wrote;
Words of great beauty never die;
Words lesser folk like me can quote
But oh! why do they make me cry?

Good too that great composers write;
Their works go singing down the years.
But as I listen with delight
Why do I find myself in tears?

Good is it that great artists paint
Masterpieces 'ere they die
That buyers' millions cannot taint
But Van Gogh's *Boots* still makes me cry.

And best of all to climb the hills;
To see the fields and woods and sky;
And if it is for human ills,
Then I am glad that I can cry!

Nancy Holt

HELP!

What can you do when the beatings start,
When the fear inside almost stops your heart.
Do you fold your arms above your head
To protect you from the blows you dread
As they land you scream in pain
Until you feel you'll go insane.
You pray to God the pain will go
But all you feel is another blow.
You watch the boots that's all you see
With head bent low you moan and plea,
A plea that's thrown into the air
Will someone help?
Will someone care?
Handsful of hair uprooted fall
As your head is smashed against a wall
One boot moves you feel a thud
You hear your voice scream, 'I'll be good,'
By now you're curled up like a ball.
You're wet with blood and tears that fall.
The bloodied boots have gone away
But they'll be back another day
Finally you're left alone
In this place called home sweet home.

Mary Jones

A HIGHER POWER

Birds are singing, she opens her eyes,
The dawn is here, it's time to rise,
After living a life of hell on earth,
Most days bring happiness and self worth.

Everyday was hard, full of strife,
Pointless and empty, angry at life.
Losing integrity, morals, control,
Void of emotion, stealing your soul.

Praying to God for guidance and peace,
Desperately wanting the misery to cease,
He took her life and changed it around,
She knew that in God a friend she had found.

Mariza Arnold

THE MAN AT THE SHANKILL

The eyes of a child
Were raised my direction,
As if to ask me why.
Why had my daddy
Been buried by rubble?
Why had they let him die?

As I choked back my sorrow
And anger within,
My answer was hard to reply
For the question put to me,
I just couldn't answer
The reason I didn't know why.

In my arms I embraced her
And offered some comfort,
Yet I knew it would never repair
The destruction and damage
The loss of his life
Her father was no longer there.

Now as months pass me by
And seasons still change,
I shall never forget her face
For the people who caused this
The pain and confusion
I feel much remorse and disgrace.

Judith McGrath

169

1994

We live in a world of bitter strife,
The value lost of human life.
We fly in space, while famine reigns,
And wars rage on for all our pains.

We know that by one little blunder,
Our universe is rent asunder.
Where is the one with spirit bold,
Who'd say the nations must be told,
To stay each one within their rights,
To stop the wars and bloody fights.
To stem the tide of power and hate,
To stop, before it is too late.

We watch with sad and wondering eye,
The children starve and people die,
Filling man's lust for power and gain,
Filling the earth with grief and pain.

Will the nations never learn,
Or are they are too blind
To realise the misery they
Bring to all mankind.
This lovely earth was made for joy,
Not for the evil to destroy.

Florence Athersmith

THEY SHALL REST IN PEACE

Higher, higher
up the hill,
At the top
we stop.

Grandparents lie in rest.
The earth here is blest.
Who would harm
their resting place?
The world condemns
such vile disgrace.

Long, long ago
we came to pray,
For their dear souls
so far away.

Rain water
washed our hands.
No taps then
at our commands.

We will see
they rest in peace,
For our watch
will never cease.

Sybil Glucksmann

GENOCIDE

Together we were born to be,
A thriving nation, people free.
Diaspora forced us to part,
And plant revenge within our hearts.

The pogroms came at us with stones
And fire, to see our scattered bones;
To throw our Jewish shells to mud,
To go to war, to shed our blood.

And many others tried the same;
Make accusations, attribute blame.
By many we have been expelled.
To fight and kill, we've been compelled.

Our plans then Hitler did impede,
And killed our nation with great speed.
A life of shame, no dignity.
Our people caught, no longer free.

Horrific fates for us agreed.
Our Jewish numbers did recede;
And by G-d's laws *we did* abide,
Yet our reward was genocide!

Bella Morris

DEDICATE YOUR POETRY

If you are an unknown poet, a trier like me. A poet who desires his/her poetry to be read then I address this article to you.
Competition for space on the bookshop-shelf is fierce. This is the operative word in today's business.
The fields of poetry and prose are in my opinion the most competitive of all.
This should not be so. But it is. A poem should be read for its worth and merits the due reward its originator deserves.
What is needed are pegs on which we hang our work.
These *pegs* must be well-known, attractive, eye catching and visible to all would be readers.
Few of us are famous or related to celebrities, so how can we achieve success? I suggest we *dedicate our work to a person who has achieved fame in his or her chosen field.*
It may be a politician or artist who would welcome your poem and give their consent to its publication.
A famous performer on the TV, stage or screen may reside in your area and be happy to have their name associated with your work.
Have your poems an element of obscurity? Do their inner meanings task the mind? If this is so, they may be of use for examination purposes or valuable for local discussion groups or evening class poetry readings.
The main thing is to keep writing and hope that one day your work will be read. Remember the painter Van Gogh was not able to sell one painting in his whole lifetime, but how I wish I could have bought just one. Yes one.

Francis Rylance

A DANCE TO THE MUSIC OF TIME

Frederick Krupp lay awake, listening.

The night had been a triumph. Aged eight, he had given his first public performance of Mozart's Piano Concerto No 21 in C Major (K.467) at the Royal Festival Hall and had received a standing ovation. The conductor's reception, too, had been impressive: mother elegant in blue silk, father immaculate in evening dress, guests too numerous and celebrated to mention other than in alphabetical order, glorious food.

Now he listened to his parents misconducting themselves in the next room. He refused to call it *'having it off'*, the phrase used by some of his more worldly and coarse school friends. He was not sure what the expression meant, but he kept rabbits and knew it involved seventeen stones of Deputy Headmaster sliding about on a mere eight and a half of Public Librarian.

His collection of tiny glass animals on the bedside table began to tinkle and shake. A horse trembled and fell and broke its leg before Frederick could save it. Eyes glistening, he turned for consolation to the score of the Fauré Requiem.

By the time the thudding and shouting died next door he was dreaming of future twin-sister musicians and the occasion of his and their magnificent rendering of Beethoven's Triple Concerto in C Minor (Op. 56).

David Clarke

BACKSTAGE TO MR BOWIE

Some years ago there was a slim paperback by the name of
'Free Spirit', with writings from David Bowie's first wife
Angela. It included an account of her relationship with the
Rock Star, and also some poetry. The personal kind which may
mean more, to the writer than a reader.

In 1980 the marriage between them ends with divorce, and David
Bowie gets custody of Zowie. There was a settlement based on
the fact that she wouldn't *"kiss and tell"*, for at least 10 years.

Well now we see a larger, thicker, and hardback version. It is
entitled *'Backstage Passes'* (Roion - £14.99). The chapters are
littered with characters and antics, in reference to a career.
Another tale of the Rock 'N' Roll story, with sleaze element in
it for good measure.

Perhaps Bowie's ex-wife should have done her homework a bit
better. She didn't even get the colour of his eyes right. More could
have been said about a period in time, we now refer to as being the
free-love decade. Nothing of any real lasting damage is thrown-up
by this publication, and it does not say anything that hasn't been said
before. Not what you would call breaking new ground.

Towards the end Angie blames Coco Schwab, for things going sour
between her and David. Coco became his Personal Assistant in a
business sense. Whether some kind of witch or very good friend,
there seems to be a special friendship - between Coco and David I
mean.

Now Bowie is married to Iman and happy again. The mystique of the
man has stayed intact, while contemporaries have fallen from grace.
Everything is 'Hunky Dory' as David would say, or not as the case
may be!

Tony Oxborough